Just Do Nothing

A PARADOXICAL GUIDE TO
GETTING OUT OF YOUR WAY

Joanna Hardis

FINN-PHYLLIS
PRESS

Just Do Nothing / Joanna Hardis —1st ed.

ISBN 979-8-9873612-5-2 (paperback)
ISBN 979-8-9873612-6-9 (eBook)

Author photograph by Emily Metzger

www.JoannaHardis.com

PRAISE FOR JUST DO NOTHING

"Practical. Friendly. Funny. As usual, Joanna knocks it out of the park with sound advice that you can actually use!"

—*Drew Linsalata, author of The Anxious Truth and Seven Percent Slower*

"Life has its ways of stressing us all out. In *Just Do Nothing*, Joanna Hardis helps us change our agenda from one of fruitlessly *fighting* the discomfort to one of *leaning into it* and relating to it better. Her amazing book takes scientifically proven cognitive-behavioral therapy strategies and blends them with her own wit, humor, illustrative case examples, and useful experiential exercises (and even a few f-bombs). You will definitely enjoy her entertaining and creative writing—but more importantly, you will benefit from Joanna's knowledge and expertise."

—*Jon Abramowitz, PhD Professor of Psychology at University of North Carolina, Chapel Hill*

To Izzy, Luke, and Josie; I really hit the karmic jackpot with the three of you. You will always be my number one.

And to the many patients I have treated; you have taught me so much. Thank you for allowing me to travel alongside you.

Disclaimer

Although the publisher and the author have made every effort to ensure that the information in this book was correct at press time, and while this publication is designed to provide accurate information in regard to the subject matter covered, the publisher and the author assume no responsibility for errors, inaccuracies, omissions, or any other inconsistencies herein and hereby disclaim any liability to any party for any loss, damage, or disruption caused by errors or omissions, whether such errors or omissions result from negligence, accident, or any other cause.

This publication is meant as a source of valuable information for the reader, however it is not meant as a substitute for direct expert assistance. If such level of assistance is required, the services of a competent professional should be sought.

Contents

CHAPTER I

How Did We Get Here?

B y "here," I'm referring to two things: the writing of this book and whatever caused you to purchase it.

First, let me tell you a bit about why I wrote this book for you.

The truth is, I never intended to write a book. People have suggested the idea in passing (like, "You should put that in a book!" or "When are you going to write that book?"), and I've always blown it off because I never thought I had anything useful to say. But then I found myself ghosted at Canyon Ranch Spa in Tucson, Arizona, on my fifty-first birthday, and suddenly, I had something to say.

Allow me to give you a bit of history so you can appreciate why this ghosting experience stung so much. After all, I'm a licensed therapist; being ghosted should be a "relatively easy" thing to deal with, right?

I'd been divorced for over ten years when this happened. To say that the end of my marriage was messy and painful would be an understatement. I recently learned that the euphemistic word for what I experienced is "relationship betrayal" (which sounds about as nice as it is). Without getting into the details, which are irrelevant at this point, I have never known pain like I did when I found out my husband had fallen for another woman. I didn't know I was capable of feeling emotions as intensely and frequently (and often unpredictably) as I did for the two years after I found out. Beyond the nightmares, flashbacks, sleepless nights, sleepy days, a brain that felt like Swiss cheese, and a lack of appetite that swiftly turned to a voracious appetite, it physically hurt to be in so much emotional pain. The grief hurt. My muscles were so tight, as I remained constantly vigilant, waiting for the other shoe to drop, that I felt like a tweaked-out squirrel (not that I know what one of those looks like) every waking moment.

Taking care of my three kids, who were with me eighty percent of the time, was my primary concern. Then work. Then getting divorced. My needs, including dating, were not a high priority. Even once I started feeling better, I didn't want to get near anything that could risk my precarious stability. I wanted a guarantee I'd never have to feel that kind of pain again. For a long time, it seemed too hard and not worth the risk.

Also, it was easier to avoid the idea of dating

again when the kids were younger. I was busy with their stuff, and weekends were filled with sports-related activities. It didn't even matter that I wasn't terribly interested in their sports; what mattered was, I had things to do! I was busy! There were always people around with whom I could have dinner and kibitz.

Things changed, however, as my kids got older. Suddenly I had time on my hands. That "free time" provided me with some freedom, which I loved, but also loneliness. Yes, I had friends, but, in my town at least, coupled friends typically don't hang with single friends on the weekends. If their husbands were away, I'd get an invitation. But generally, between Thursday and Sunday, they were booked. I was lonely. And suddenly, the scales shifted, and the side that held and the potential upside of dating became heavier.

Acknowledging that the possible rewards of dating might outweigh the potential risks, I decided I had to take some action. In my ideal world, I would be set up by trusted friends. The person would be well vetted, their history scoured for sketchiness and red (and yellow) flags, delivered ready-to-date. In the end, I *was* set up a few times, but more times than not it was with someone my friends didn't really know, so it didn't get very far.

As much as I resisted it, I eventually put my profile on some dating apps. It was profoundly disturbing to think that my clients or prospective clients could see my dating profile, but this is (apparently) what modern dating looks like. As an introvert, I've determined that the way one has to date these days to successfully find love online may be an undocumented stage of purgatory. All the funneling necessary to find a few good men is exhausting. But I digress. (And, for the record, I've dated some amazing men I've met online.)

I had been dating for several years when I met "the ghoster." At the time, things *seemed* different. We had an easy vibe, what seemed like similar interests, and a commitment to open communication (which now seems laughable). It appeared that we were aligned in seeing where this could go. For the first time in a while, I allowed myself to have hope. Oh how intoxicating a drug that can be.

We had been dating for a few months when I invited him to meet me in Tucson for my birthday weekend. I would be going out for the full week, and he would meet me for the tail end. But three days before I left, without explanation, he ceased all contact.

When I left for Tucson on Tuesday, I was pretty sure I was being ghosted, although I had the tiniest sliver of hope he might still show up. Up until my departure, I was a wreck as I rode the emotional roller coaster, wondering if he was going to call or not. Without warning, that familiar pain I had when my marriage fell apart came back: tightness in my chest, my stomach clenching, the lump in my throat, and trouble getting a deep enough breath. HOW DID THIS

HAPPEN? HOW DID I MISS THE SIGNS? HOW COULD I BE SO STUPID? I CANNOT DO THIS AGAIN. THIS CAN'T BE HAPPENING. *WHAT THE FUCK!*

The noise in my head was deafening. My head throbbed. My body clenched as if I had just been punched in the gut. Every muscle was tense, bracing for impact as I tortured myself with unanswerable questions and self-blame. Well-intentioned people would later try to cheer me up, hoping to ease the pain with platitudes like "Wow, you're so lucky to have dodged a real bullet" and "It's not about you, it's about him." While I understood that I wasn't the emotionally immature one who bailed, it sure *seemed* to be about me as I crawled out of my skin with confusion.

I knew, even as the plane began its journey toward Tucson, that there would be lots of moments when I would feel like shit. I wish I could write that, while on vacation, I met the sweetest, funniest, totally jacked empath who loved me more than his daily Pangram game. But I didn't. I also wish that I could write that that's the week I learned to love myself unconditionally. But it wasn't. The week was hard AF. I referred to it as a "working vacation" since I was working hard not to torpedo the entire seven days by living in my head. I've done that way too many times.

The question was: did I want to guarantee a terrible time by staying in bed ruminating while feeling like shit (which was all I wanted to do), or would I go do the things I loved and see how I felt (which would likely be shitty, but I wouldn't know for sure unless I tried)?

I knew it was pointless to try to *force* myself to be happy by "looking on the bright side" or "finding the silver lining." I knew there would be silver linings to this experience, but it was too early and I was still in too much pain to see them. I will confess that the low point of the week, hands down, was when the front desk called on my birthday to ask if he would be coming. With Beyonce's "Lemonade" playing in the background, I replied, "That MOFO ghosted me a week ago, so I'm betting not."

To this day, I've never heard from him. And no, he's not dead. I checked.

I had enough lived experience by that point to know that it didn't matter if I liked what was happening to me or why it was happening. None of that could change the reality that it *was* happening. In fact, the more I fought that reality, the worse I felt.

There wasn't some magical moment in the desert when everything suddenly made sense. The universe didn't speak to me. No one said anything "that resonated to my core." I didn't have an epiphany at an ayahuasca ceremony or get wisdom from a shaman. Those would make for cooler stories, but as my luck would have it, nothing dramatic enough to make for a great story transpired. But, while on a run, the briefest moment of clarity did strike (maybe that was the universe, after all).

In that brief moment, I realized I knew how to get through this. I didn't need to research ghosting, schedule a session with an astrologer, call my therapist, go to a talk, or exercise the toxins out. I didn't need to figure anything out, I didn't need to understand anything, and I didn't need to know how the story would end. I didn't need to *do* anything. This problem was not going to be fixed by doing. I was going to get through this by *allowing*. Namely, allowing reality to unfold as it would, and, toward that end, feeling a lot of feelings.

Because I'd been speaking on these sorts of painful experiences and how to navigate them for years, I knew that the less time I spent fighting my thoughts and feelings, the faster they would pass. I thought of myself like a snow globe that had been shaken up and simply needed to settle. The snow represented distress and discomfort, emotions I know well, both personally and professionally. My entire career has been predicated on helping people shift their relationship with some form of distress or discomfort. And that moment of awareness while jogging through the dry desert gave me the foothold I needed to pull myself out. Happy birthday to me.

From that moment on, I engaged in activities *while* I felt sad, mad, rejected, alone, pathetic, frustrated, happy, ambivalent, and uncertain. You name it, I felt it. But instead of avoiding life because I felt like shit, I brought those feelings with me as I engaged.

There were of course times when I would have had more fun on my couch binging "Succession," but more often than not, it felt better to be out of my house and out of my head. The goal wasn't to be happy, per se (although I would have loved it had that been the immediate outcome). The goal was to do the process of discomfort differently since that's all I could control.

As I write this, that particular experience is many months behind me. Some days have been easier than others. If I'm tired, hungry, lonely, stressed, or feeling overwhelmed, thoughts of him and what happened are likely to be stickier. I might get bogged down with thoughts like *How could someone be so duplicitous? Is he a sociopath?* or *How could I have been so stupid?* I'm much better at pulling myself out of these spirals than I used to be, but my healing has not been linear. No one's is. At times, he's had more mental real estate than he deserves, but I've also been quicker to evict thoughts of him than I was previously. Additionally, knowing the risks of avoiding the discomfort allowed me to start dating again more quickly than I might have otherwise.

As I look back more generally on my post-divorce life over the past decade, the game changer was learning that I didn't have to be ready or motivated in order to do new things. I only had to be willing. "I'm not ready" was the lie I told myself to avoid all sorts of things. There have been many excuses I've used to talk myself out of taking action:

The criteria were not exactly how I envisioned them. For example, I didn't leave a job I hated for years to start my own practice because I couldn't find the perfect office space. Or, I didn't date guys who were under six feet tall (I'm only five feet tall, so this made no logical sense). Once, I was offered to teach a graduate-level class, but I turned it down because it was virtual and I felt it was too confusing (this was pre-Covid).

I had to do "just a little more research" in order to change. I can recall two houses I missed out on because I had to do more "research" to make the best bid. I have agonized over so many decisions that, looking back, didn't really matter, including, but not limited to, wedding planning, how long to breastfeed (and whether to breastfeed), giving a newborn a pacifier, and on and on (I won't bore you with any more of them!).

I didn't think I could handle it. (Not that I had any idea of what the "it" was; I just knew I couldn't handle it.)

I didn't think it was "in me" to do hard things; I wasn't brave or strong. Somewhere along the way, I developed a story that I was a worrier, and that worriers are not brave or strong.

The belief that you can do hard things is called self-efficacy, and mine, post-divorce, was less than zero. In some cases through necessity and in others through choice, I learned what's actually possible, whether in the area of dating, powerlifting, starting my own business, leaving a field I had been in for thirteen years, raising three kids as a single parent, vacationing alone with my kids, doing college drop off and pick up alone, making hard decisions alone, vacationing alone, or writing this book, to name but a few. Slowly, I started seeing myself as someone who could handle things. I don't think I would have ever realized how much I'm truly capable of handling had I not decided to take a lot of chances. Again, some by choice, some because there was no other option.

Also, I don't think I fully realized how much ground I covered and how much more successful I became in the area of handling uncomfortable situations *until* I was ghosted, and, while not the most pleasant experience on the planet, it didn't take me down nearly as hard or for nearly as long as it would have a decade ago. There is no better teacher than experience. Experience taught me that I can do hard things. They may suck, but I can do them. And if I can do them, so can you.

So that's why I wrote this book. As for why you picked up this book, I'm guessing that you're feeling like there's a space between where you are now and where you want to be.

Maybe you want to be a badass, listen to your inner warrior, be more hardcore, and do some things differently, but something keeps getting in your way.

Maybe you spend too much time in your head. Maybe you panic when things start to feel "too much." Maybe your solutions end up becoming your problems. Maybe you feel like you've been this way so long that you can't ever change. Maybe you bail whenever things begin to feel too uncomfortable. I get it. (Maybe not the inner warrior stuff, but all the rest.)

I know where you are. You've read the self-help books, listened to the podcasts, made endless pro and con lists, maybe even gone to some weekend workshops, but it still seems like you struggle to execute on all those go-get-'em-tiger messages on your Lululemon bag or recently purchased motivational coffee mug. You know the sayings I'm talking about: "Get comfortable being uncomfortable," "Do one thing a day that scares you," "Be a badass," "Live fearlessly."

Maybe now is as good a time as any to interject that I have many pet peeves, two of which are particularly relevant to this book: word art and vapid inspirational quotes—*especially* when paired. Do we really need a wall hanging that says, "It's Wine O'Clock Somewhere?" (Yes, it is the title of chapter 7, but using it ironically is fun.) Do we need a front doormat that reminds us to "Live Laugh Love"? Pet Peeve number three: toxic positivity. Sadly, we frequently see vapid, "toxically positive" messages written with word art, and I have a visceral reaction to the threefold combination every single time. *Good Vibes Only! Don't Worry, Be Happy! Choose Happiness! Positivity Only! Vibrate High!*

Let me be clear—I am not anti-happiness and good vibes. What I find problematic is the message that we *shouldn't* feel the full range of feelings and that some are bad, not to be felt. Just because you think it, doesn't mean it's true. Similarly, just because your mug or wall art says it, doesn't mean it's true or, if it is, that you understand how to truly embody it!

Therefore, I decided to have a bit of fun and title each chapter of this book based on a common inspirational quote that is often spouted with good intentions, but either isn't backed by science or doesn't teach a human being to actually take the next best steps toward their goals (or both).

Further, none of the changes you are hoping for will show up and become commonplace simply by reading about them or reciting a mantra here and there. You want to listen to your inner badass self, so you purchase a book (or six) on how to do so. But how many times do you finish the book on how to do what you want to do or be who you want to be, but then two weeks later you find yourself back in the same place you started? Or, you got hyped up by the workshop you attended, but then had no clue *how* to get started and implement the shifts necessary to unhook from your old stories and (finally) get out of your own way? The steps often make so much sense in your head, but when you attempt to actually *do* them, you realize that you don't actually know what to do. And, if you're like me, you likely beat yourself up for not being able to do it. It feels like you should know how, or your friends seem to know how, or someone directly alluded to the idea that there's something wrong with you because you *don't* know how.

Through the course of this book, I'm going to help you navigate two core principles that are backed by science to help you get unstuck and out of your own way so you can do the hard stuff you want to do. When it comes to the "stuff" in our heads (and by that, I mean our thoughts, feelings, and sensations), we need to *do the opposite of what's intuitive*.

This is precisely why this book's title is *Just Do Nothing*. When we encounter distress or discomfort, it's intuitive to try to *do* something to either avoid it or eradicate it in some way. As you'll learn, however, that only makes it stronger and more persistent. To make it pass, we want to face the situation and give the thoughts and feelings as little attention as possible. To do that, we're going to need to learn how to interact differently with our internal experience. That's what this book will teach you how to do: learn how to tolerate distress.

We may know *what* to do when things get hard, but we don't know *how* to do it. Therefore, all of our attempts to get rid of our distress and discomfort are actually making things worse and getting in the way of change. To tolerate distress, we must learn how to relax into it.

By the end of this book, you'll have an

understanding of how to turn "I can't" into "I can't…*yet*" so you can make the changes you want to make and finally feel like the badass you absolutely are.

ACTION STEP

Identify one of your primary "can'ts" and rewrite it as "I can't _____ *yet*."

HOW TO USE THIS BOOK

Having a lot of Virgo placements in my birth chart means I tend to be detail-oriented and thorough, generally to an annoying degree. Toward this end, I have tried to convey the information in this book in as clear, concise, and useful a way as possible.

How you choose to consume the book is up to you. You might choose to read it all the way through, read a chapter, and then work on the exercises before proceeding, or do only the exercises. (I don't recommend the latter, because the exercises won't make as much sense without the content from the associated chapter.)

My recommendation is to read each chapter and then do the exercise at the end. Each chapter, ideally, builds on the previous one and has a mixture of nerdy science stuff (which I love) and practical application (that all-important explanation of *how* you can incorporate it into your life).

In case you're a skimmer, here's the TL;DR (Too Long; Didn't Read): Each chapter ends with a mental fitness skill (from my accumulated list of such practices) for doing hard stuff and having quality mental health. **These skills are meant to be practiced as often as you possibly can. We cannot lay new neural pathways, which is what we are trying to do, without a TON of practice and repetition. I cannot stress this enough.** If you want to be a great tennis player, you can read every book on the game of tennis, watch every video on how to serve like Serena, or go to every tennis match the world over, but until you start playing, you are not a tennis *player*. Simply reading this book is a great start, but let's raise the bar for "working on yourself" to a level that gives you a fighting chance of truly feeling better for the long term.

If you want to stop overthinking and letting your feelings control you, it will require *intentional* practice and repetition. Not only will I lay out the skills and instructions on how to practice those skills, but you'll also have an opportunity to plan how/when you'll practice out in the real world. We can't create new learning if we don't do the action and give ourselves every possibility for success. It is metabolically inefficient for our brains to do anything (meaning that it takes a lot of energy for our brains to do what they don't automatically do), which is another reason it's so hard to change. If we want to change, we have to give our brains lots of reminders and put in a lot of effort to make it happen.

"Change begins at the end of your comfort zone" is all the rage, but what's missing is the endnote that says, "Also, it will take a bit longer and be a tad more challenging than the effort required simply to read the quote!"

Post-it Notes will be your best friend. My recommendation is to practice each skill for a week until you move on to the next. Practice them at different times of day, in different settings, and while in different moods to get a sense of where you feel more competent and what areas need more targeted practice. And remember, these are life skills. You, like me, will be practicing them for the rest of your life.

Finally, at the end of each chapter is a blank page for you to record your wins. Change is made up of many micro-shifts in behavior, so it's important to start spotting them and treating them as deposits in your confidence (or change) bank. Big changes are often as exciting as taking an exotic vacation, because they don't happen all that often. Small changes, however, happen all the time, and we need to be better about noticing and celebrating them. Don't skip this part! Write down your wins, both big and small. It'll help to be able to refer back to them on tougher days when you fear you aren't making much progress.

LET'S CHAT ABOUT MINDSET

Remember how much you fumbled when you

first learned how to drive? Are you still driving like that? I hope not.

Any time we're learning something new, we're going to be clumsy and uncomfortable at first. It's not going to be a pretty sight for 99.9% of us. We accept that as part of the process. Any time you've attempted something new, the more you did it (whatever "it" was), the easier it surely got. You didn't assume that the way you drove the first month was the way you'd always drive.

This is no different. It's going to be confusing at first. You're not going to "get it" right away. You're going to tell yourself you should be able to do it better more quickly, or you're going to attempt it and immediately declare, "It didn't work." The principles may seem simple, but they are not easy to implement, especially in moments when you feel distress. It requires patience, compassion, curiosity, and a good sense of humor.

Over the course of my career, I've had the honor of working with many incredible clients who gave me the best education I could ever ask for. From the HIV/AIDS unit at the county hospital to over a decade in an eating disorder treatment center to now running my own practice, I have learned from an incredible bunch. In that time, I've reflected a lot about what most helps someone make lasting change.

8 NECESSARY INGREDIENTS FOR LASTING CHANGE

(and the chapter where I tackle each)

- Celebrating small wins (end of each chapter plus chapter 11)
- Redefining your relationship with failure (chapter 11)
- Treating self-compassion as a skill to be practiced (chapter 12)
- Responding to yourself without judgment (chapters 5 and 6)
- Practicing distress tolerance (chapter 9)
- Practicing allowing (chapter 9)
- Separating facts from meaning-making of your thoughts and feelings (chapters 5 and 6)
- Taking your focus off the outcome (chapters 3, 9, and 11-20)

So, are you ready? First things first, let's talk about what behavior change really is, and why you've struggled with it thus far. (Trust me, this is going to give you a good bit of relief if you're someone who's quick to beat yourself up for not following through on a commitment to change.)

CHAPTER 2

"Do One Thing Each Day That Scares You."

Our brains were designed to avoid pain, detect risk, and keep us alive. We're wired to notice what's wrong, not what's right (this is known as negativity bias). Our desire to avoid distress and discomfort makes complete sense—*if* we're actually in danger. But what if the fear isn't actually happening? What if it just feels real or important or yucky or unpleasant or uncomfortable or impossible? If you're like *so* many others, you may be reacting to how you feel or what could happen versus what's actually in front of you. When we're worked up, we move faster, lock in, and put all our resources into feeling better, safer, or more certain. It makes intuitive sense, but it also may be getting in the way of you getting what you want. I've seen it over and over again in my practice, and I've certainly experienced it in my own life.

Have you ever left your favorite fitness class hopped up on inspiration about "slaying" and the notion that "breakthroughs on the bike equal breakthroughs in life!" only to find yourself binge-watching "Real Housewives" a few hours later, having slayed nothing other than your snack cabinet? I can't be the only one.

It's not that you don't know what you want to do (or are supposed to do) but simply can't get yourself to do it. It's not that you're lazy or lack willpower. It's just that, when the inspo-glow wears off and you think about actually doing "the thing," you get that familiar feeling of dread—the swirling in your stomach or the buzzing in your head. Then, all of a sudden, you're bombarded by a million ways the action you want to take could go horribly wrong and/or why today isn't the right day to do it. You go back and forth in your head, waffling between "do I or don't I?" and the more you waffle, the bigger the feeling gets until you've had it, at which point you declare, "Not today, Satan" and watch another episode or pour yourself some wine. You've concluded that the "risks" aren't worth it. You're not up for it. It's one more thing you "can't handle."

For many of us, this pattern doesn't stop after one instance. One instance turns into two, three, and four until you've given up on the goal completely and once again berated yourself for screwing up (again). As if this weren't bad enough, the experience then becomes yet another repetitive chapter in your story of not being able to change or do hard things.

Perhaps your experience is that you know what you want to do, but when you consider doing it, your body feels like it has another plan. This basically described my relationship with sports growing up. When I was a kid, my parents decided to enroll me in tennis lessons. I was the youngest of my siblings, raised in the '70s, and there was absolutely no such thing as helicopter parenting at that time (not that my mother would have subscribed to it anyway).

My parents played tennis, and there were courts down the street (and therefore summer camps) so I was enrolled. Because they worked full-time, I had to be occupied for many hours each day, so I took a lot of lessons and went to a lot of camps. I got reasonably good while in practice, but the minute I got near a competitive situation, my body freaked out. As a kid, I had no idea about the fight or flight response or anxiety attacks. I just knew I experienced a familiar pattern before matches—waves of adrenaline, my stomach in knots, fighting back the urge to vomit, and a huge lump in my throat as my brain served me one worried, negative, self-critical thought after another. Once I missed a single shot, it was "game over." I choked, and nothing—and I mean nothing—went over the net after that point. This happened over and over again. My coaches and parents kept telling me to just relax, which only made things worse. I left every match an angry, frustrated, anxious mess. Pressure was not my friend.

The same thing happened when I had to take the SAT. Looking back, I'm fairly certain I struggled with Generalized Anxiety Disorder throughout my late childhood and adolescence, but it wasn't officially diagnosed until I was well into adulthood. All I knew was that on the day of the SAT, I woke up nauseous, couldn't keep food down, had trouble focusing, and was embarrassingly sweaty. It's no wonder my scores were terrible. I'm not sure if I'm truly a terrible test taker, but that was the explanation that was given. I know that *standardized* tests are not my jam, but without the raging panic, would I suck as much as I did? Who knows. Nevertheless, the story persisted that I'm not someone who likes pressure or competition. Even today, something as trivial as a board game can be stressful for me if the other players are super intense about winning. My initial response in all of these situations is that I can't handle it or it's not worth it or it's too much, so I bail.

In the therapy world, we would say I was exhibiting distress intolerance in those situations. Clinically speaking, according to the National Library of Medicine, distress tolerance is the (a) the *perceived* capacity to withstand negative emotional and/or other aversive states (e.g., physical discomfort), and (b) the *behavioral act* of withstanding distressing internal states elicited by some type of stressor.

In layman's terms, distress intolerance is the

perception that you cannot handle unpleasant feelings or sensations, so you avoid them. Distress *tolerance*, therefore, is someone's perception that they *can* handle negative internal states and behavior that matches (in other words, not avoiding them in any way). We all have instances where we are distress intolerant. It's extremely important that you understand that being distress intolerant, in the clinical sense, involves having a *pattern* of avoidance based on the perception that you can't handle the feelings. It's not a one-time thing. In the field, we think of distress tolerance/intolerance as a construct or a tool to understand behavior. We wouldn't use it to describe a one-off behavior but instead to describe patterns.

So, for our purposes, I am talking about a *pattern* of talking yourself out of doing things because you think you can't handle difficult or aversive internal states, and that pattern is getting in the way of you doing hard stuff.

Whether you are distress tolerant/intolerant in any given situation, therefore, is determined by your *perception* of whether you can handle a particular feeling, followed by the behavioral consequence. That consequence could be going about your day while feeling the uncomfortable feeling (distress tolerance) or escaping, avoiding, procrastinating, or busting out a bottle of wine at noon after rationalizing that it's "five o'clock somewhere" (distress intolerance).

Here are some examples of how distress

*in*tolerance may sound:

- "I can't bear this (perception) so I'm leaving (action)."
- "I can't stand this feeling (perception) so I'm going to have a beer (action)."
- "It takes so much to get going (perception), it's just not worth the effort so I cancel (action)."
- "It has to stop (perception) so I'm going to bed for the rest of the day (action)."
- "This is too much (perception) so I'm done (action)."
- "It felt so real (perception), I had to figure it out (action)."
- "The anxiety will ruin my entire day (perception) so I'm going to work from home today (action)."
- "I can't cope (perception) so I'm just going to tell you everything is fine (action)."
- "I don't know how people do it, but I can't (perception), so I don't date online (action)."
- "F*** it, I'm done (action), I've had it (perception)."
- "I know I should do it, but I can't (perception), so I put it off (action)."
- "My feelings last forever (perception) so I avoid things that get me worked up (action)."

In all of these examples, the solution (in other words, the action) eventually became the problem. Let that sink in for a second. What we do, *what we think is helping*, eventually becomes our real problem. The leaving, avoiding, drinking, sleeping, overthinking, shutting down, or procrastinating—all the coping behaviors I'll lay out further in chapter 7—become the problem. And, ironically, we generally do those things to avoid feeling something unpleasant or uncomfortable.

If you're anything like me, you may be freaking out that you've said nearly all of them (if not every single one) of the above statements and conclude that you're hopelessly fucked up. This is absolutely not the case. The fact that you've uttered those words or avoided certain behaviors or activities means nothing.

What's important to consider is:

- Is this a pattern of behavior for me?
- Is it getting in the way of what I want or where I want to be?
- What's the cost of doing it (in terms of time and energy)?

The idea of distress intolerance is not binary (it's not all or nothing). Think of it as existing on a continuum from more tolerant to less tolerant. At one end of the spectrum is mildly intolerant and at the other is clinically significant intolerance. Within a single day, you may fluctuate between more and less tolerant. There are a lot of factors that impact your distress tolerance, including how much sleep you've had, whether you're hungover, hungry, stressed out, exhausted, pre-menstrual, or experiencing other hormonal swings.

If your relationship with unpleasant feelings is one of "must avoid and get rid of," I'm speaking directly to you when I say, "You're not alone." Not by a long shot. Most of the country, if not the world, is in the same boat. You're just aware of it now. The cool thing is, there are things we can do to stretch and strengthen our tolerance muscles. And, like heavy weight training (I'm a powerlifter, so prepare yourself for that analogy to keep presenting itself), when done correctly, the benefits generally outweigh the risks.

This piece of our puzzle, our distress tolerance muscle, is actually *really* important. There's a good bit of data that links distress intolerance as a risk factor in the development and maintenance of multiple mental health challenges, such as substance use disorders, depressive disorders, and anxiety disorders. Think about it. If you grew up learning (unintentionally) that feeling uncomfortable or unpleasant feelings is scary, shameful, painful, or in some other way not supported and encouraged, you'll likely now find some way to make the distress stop. If it happens over and over, it'll probably become a patterned behavior, and the carved-out pathway will become a paved road. In a very simplified way, that's how avoidance, numbing out, and being chronically stressed out and worried can become our default coping "skills," and how bigger challenges can develop (in other words, the solution becomes the problem). And, on a very practical level, constantly working to get rid of negative internal states creates a lot of unnecessary (and potentially unhealthy) work to manage.

I had a client who, when she was little, was always worried her younger brother would leave his soccer ball by the furnace and the house would blow up. She'd get nervous before bed and start checking the furnace to make sure it was unobstructed, thinking that would keep any fires from starting as everyone slept. Within a couple of years, her fire fears crept to the stove, water heater, appliances, outlets, wires, anything close to radiators, and so on. The list of things she had to check grew with each new possibility. And, her process wasn't restricted to simply checking. She would also call her parents for reassurance, replay her steps in her head to make sure she checked everything, and eventually even took pictures for confirmation that everything was off, unplugged, and in place.

Transitioning to college was a nightmare since the fears persisted, but she couldn't ever feel like things were safe enough. It was like an itch she couldn't stop scratching. She was driving her parents crazy with all her calls for reassurance and making sure they were okay. The only thing her brain knew to do when it got "that feeling" (distress) was to furiously check the house, scour her memories, or call her parents. It was a vicious cycle of having a scary thought, feeling pan-icked, and checking or seeking reassurance to try to feel better. Eventually, the distress (and her inability to tolerate it effectively) started interfering with her school and social life, and she had to take a semester off to get treatment. In short, she had to learn how to live with uncertainty again.

In this example, it's easy to see how her world shrank as her worries grew. By the time she left for col-lege, she didn't believe she could have a thought about her parents' safety or fall asleep without calling them to confirm they were okay. At the beginning of treat-ment, she would say, "But when the thoughts happen, they feel so real and important. Ignoring them feels ir-responsible and dangerous."

I believed that the feelings felt real to her because they were paired with so much adrenaline, but that didn't mean the situation was real or dangerous. In or-der for her to build her distress tolerance back up, she had to learn how to *do distress differently*. Instead of re-acting as if there were real and present danger, she learned to slow down, step back, and take her time so she could respond to the situation, not her emotions. Then, she could *allow* the distress while she carried on with her day, went to bed, or did whatever else she was doing.

The focus wasn't on feeling better, and the as-sumption wasn't that there was anything wrong. The singular hard thing she learned to do was allow her discomfort to be there and carry on anyway. That's how you get comfortable being uncomfortable.

Another time when distress intolerance might be at play is when we're feeling stuck, because weak distress tolerance muscles can actually *keep* us stuck. One area where I see this a lot is in our relationships. You can substitute daughter, sister, wife, grandmother, partner, boss, or anyone else with whom you have a significant relationship for "kids" in the next example.

When my kids are struggling, everything I know about parenting goes out the window. I know these situations go best when I keep my mouth shut and stay calm, even if I'm storming inside. If they're in pain, my initial instinct is to swoop in, solve the problem, and try to make them feel better. It doesn't matter that I *hate* when my mother does this to me. It pains me to a large degree to see my kids so upset.

So, impulsively, I open my mouth and tell them exactly what they should do, which annoys the shit out of them. So before long, they're struggling *and* annoyed with me. Why do I open my mouth? Because of how I feel (distress). My unsolicited advice is an attempt to regulate my internal discomfort when what I need to do is accept my feelings and keep my mouth shut (in other words, strengthen my distress tolerance muscle).

People often wonder, "Was I just born this way?" As is the case in so many areas, there is rarely only one cause of something. Why we show up the way we do is multifactorial (there are multiple factors at play). In terms of distress tolerance or intolerance, we believe there are biological, environmental, and learned elements that cause someone to become distress intolerant. People who are more emotionally or physiologically sensitive (which is a real thing; people are not always just being "too sensitive" or "too much") will feel these things more easily and more intensely, and it will take longer for them to come back down to their baseline. Given the way they're wired, they will experience feelings as "sucking more" or otherwise more painful, and their efforts to avoid or get rid of them may be more intense.

The environmental piece is what happens around you—what gets modeled, what works, and what doesn't—which ties in with the learned piece. Our brains learn by association. If we're worried that our headache is brain cancer, and we ask Dr. Google (and find out it's unlikely), Dr. Google gets paired with anxiety reduction (anxious → Google → feel better temporarily). If that solves your problem, great. But if your brain comes back with another question (and another and another), you could be going down the Google and Reddit rabbit holes for hours. From that point forward, every time you get worried and, as a result, start googling, that association or pathway in your brain gets stronger.

I'm not suggesting this is *the only* reason you can't do hard stuff or why your challenges feel so difficult, but it may very well be a contributing factor. For many, being distress intolerant keeps them stuck spinning their wheels even though they know it doesn't work. Or, it may be that you want to change, but when the heat is on, you tell yourself you can't handle it and bail.

And, yes, you can be more tolerant of some emotions and sensations than others. You can also be more tolerant in some situations than others. Further, our tolerance can change from moment to moment. Most people get more intolerant as the day goes on. Late afternoon or early evening is when the "fuck its" are most likely to take over. But in order to do hard stuff, we need to know how to allow that discomfort (without making it worse) so that we can do what matters. So our can'ts become can't *yets*.

To be perfectly clear, I'm by no means suggesting that every time you do or don't do something, it has to do with being distress (in)tolerant. I don't believe that everything can be reduced to "I have distress intolerance," nor do I believe one engages in therapy for distress intolerance because they can't resist urges to scratch their feet. But I do think it's an important and often-overlooked piece of the puzzle, so let's learn how to spot it. A useful question to ask yourself is, "What the func?" which comes from Susan David's book, *Emotional Agility*. You ask it in relation to the intent of your behavior.

Let's take checking in on someone's location as an example. If the function (the "func") of checking is to reduce your fear about where they are and who they might be with, that's different from checking because someone is supposed to pick you up, it's raining out, and you're therefore wondering if they're close enough that you need to grab an umbrella. The first approach may serve to keep worry going, while the second may serve to keep you dry!

Another example is holding back during workouts. If the function of holding back is to honor that today is your recovery day, that is very different from holding back due to a perception that you can't handle sprinting because *What if I have a heart attack?* If this is the only instance where you hold yourself back (and you don't have significant fitness goals), it's probably not an issue. But if you have or develop a pattern of holding yourself back during workouts for fear of something bad happening if you push yourself, those thoughts may keep you from reaching your fitness goals. Or, they could lead to you developing health worries or cause you to start avoiding hard workouts and create a story that you don't do hard workouts because you could have a heart attack (or some other ailment).

"Do one thing every day that scares you" is incredibly inspirational. However, I've never seen any of the peppy influencers who give me my daily dose of "You can do this, Joanna" ever talk about *how* to be comfortable being uncomfortable. And we need to talk about this, because every time we give in to those itches, metaphorically speaking, or immediately check our phone or bail on a workout for (unsubstantiated) fear that we'll pass out on the treadmill, we're sending the message to our brain that the urgent feeling is important, which is precisely why we get more of them. Every time we do this dance, those neurons are firing and wiring together, making the loop stronger. We need a different way.

MENTAL FITNESS SKILL #1

WTF? What's the Func (of my behavior)?

Thinking about behaviors functionally and non-judgmentally is an incredibly helpful skill. Next time you do something—and that something could be anything from grabbing another handful of salt and vinegar potato chips (just me?) to bailing on a dinner date—pause and ask yourself, "What is my intention in doing this behavior?" **When you can identify what's driving the behavior, that's the behavior's function.** Can you identify any behaviors you engaged in where the function was to avoid distress or discomfort?

Here are a few examples to get you started:

- *Behavior*: Came home from work and grabbed a snack; *Function* of the snack: relieve hunger
- *Behavior*: Long day of seeing clients, and now

watching two episodes of "Real Housewives"; *Function* of TV watching: zone out and relax

- *Behavior*: Came home from a terrible date and ate a big bowl of ice cream; *Function* of the behavior: self-medicating sadness, loneliness
- *Behavior*: Worried about my kids, and started cleaning the house; *Function* of the behavior: try to get rid of the worry

Remember, there is no right or wrong answer. The intent is to be non-judgmental. You are trying to understand the function of your behavior so you can determine if it's effective or ineffective. Don't overthink it, and don't judge it; simply observe it.

Record Your Wins: Start training yourself to notice the small stuff, those micro-shifts in what you're noticing and how you're responding.

WINS

Write down your wins, both big and small. It'll help to be able to refer back to them on tougher days when you fear you aren't making much progress.

CHAPTER 3

"Slay the Whole Damn Day."

I've already let you in on three of my pet peeves, so allow me to reveal a fourth: the hoopla around New Year resolutions, especially the "New Year, New You" marketing craze. It drives me nuts because it's predicated on the belief that you're so messed up that you need a new you.

We frequently hear things like:

- "It's January 1, and I'm going to start meditating for ninety minutes per day, eat vegan, and do CrossFit five days a week."
- "I'm going to stop taking everything so seriously, be fully present in every moment, and work on my self-esteem."
- "I'm going to get that fifty pounds off by April so

I can do all the things I've been putting off all these years."

There's so much "wrong" with these goals when they're lumped together this way, but I hear them *all* the time. People bite off way more than they can chew and then feel discouraged when they don't make quick progress. I too have gotten hyped up about a program I saw on Instagram, bought it, and then never got past the first video. Given my other commitments, I have minimal time to invest in something new despite how interesting and helpful it appears. I *want* the results, I *want* to engage in the program, *and* it often isn't compatible with my current life circumstances. Any time I jump from being hyped up to immediately taking action, I bypass several stages in the change process (see Theoretical Model of Change below), which contributes to the action not lasting and my feeling disappointed in myself for being so impulsive, yet again.

I'm not, therefore, supportive of declarations to embark toward sweeping change all at once. What I *am* for, on the other hand, is realistic self-improvement, whether you embark on it on January 1 or August 17.

I can't argue that outcomes are sexy. Who doesn't want the prize? Whether it's being badass, fit, optimized, mindful, fearless, or finishing a marathon, outcomes sell. Where I come in is the part where you get real about the process by which to get there.

THE TRANSTHEORETICAL MODEL OF CHANGE

The Transtheoretical Model of Change was developed by psychologists Prochaska and DiClemente in the early 1980s to describe five stages of change. *Note: we don't always go through them in order.* The stages are:

- Pre-contemplation (I don't need to change)
- Contemplation (I may need to change but I'm ambivalent)
- Preparation (getting ready—getting educated about it, letting my support system know for accountability, making moves)
- Action (repetition and consistency)
- Maintenance (constantly tweaking process, making small shifts, keeping the behavior going)

Lapse (and possibly relapse) is a predictable part of change, and you may re-enter at a different stage. In other words, after you have a lapse or a relapse, you don't go all the way back to the pre-contemplation stage. You can re-enter the process at a different stage of change. You may relapse, then realize you need more preparation, so you (re)enter at the stage of preparation. Or you may re-enter at the contemplation stage if you realize you may not be as ready to change as you thought. Or perhaps you go back to the action stage if what you recognize you need more of is practice.

Despite what your favorite influencer may say (or how easy they make it look), there are so many reasons it may be difficult to change.

Here are just a few:

- You may be neuro-atypical and, therefore, much of the popular self-help materials aren't geared towards you.
- You don't have the financial resources to access the help/resources you need.
- You may not have the environment around you to support the change you desire to make.
- You may not feel safe to change in your current environment.
- You may focus exclusively on the negative possibilities and exclude any positive possibilities.
- Your goals are too big and unrealistic for starting out.
- You don't know what to do with your inner critic.
- You don't know what to do when you inevitably feel like giving up.
- You're changing for others and not for yourself.

I'm sure you can add your own to this list, and I encourage you to jot your thoughts down. In my life and work, I see a common pattern. You make the commitment to change, a commitment to do "x." You get hyped-up and think, "THIS IS IT! *I'm going to do it this time!*" Maybe you joined a Facebook group or are following someone new on Instagram or TikTok, but this time, you're ALL IN and pumped to get started.

You start the new behavior (or move toward it), and things go well for a little while. But then, inevitably, things get hard. (It always gets hard. Comfort Zones and Growth Zones are aptly named for a reason.) Whether it's keeping up the routine; the discipline of doing (or not doing) the new behavior while experiencing emotions you've been avoiding; pushing yourself emotionally, physically, and spiritually; experiencing the ripple effects of your new behaviors as your support system responds (possibly upsetting others as you learn to set boundaries) or something else, you'll eventually hit that line in the sand you'll struggle to cross. This may be the line you struggle to cross every time, or it may be a new experience for you. Regardless, the line is that place at which you tell yourself you can't do it. It's the line at which you quit.

Hitting that line may sound like:

- "Being single (or being in this relationship or this job) isn't that bad." ("The devil you know versus the devil you don't")
- "Not today, maybe tomorrow."
- "These feelings feel so intense, so real, it must mean something (so I'll stop)."
- "I really need to be more motivated (or ready) to do it."

- "I don't want to rock the boat by doing it. It's fine, I don't have to."
- "If I skip just this once it's not a big deal (but also, it's never just once)."
- "I just don't see myself as a [insert description or type of person]."
- "I just need to think about it some more, maybe ask some more people before jumping in."
- "I don't want to ruin the rest of my day if it doesn't go well."
- "I don't want to ruin anyone else's day if it doesn't go well."

Each time this pattern repeats, you lose another bit of hope that you *can* change and that things can be different. And, in all likelihood, your inner critic is loud and strong with judgment and self-criticism. I've been there, in my own self-imposed prison.

And I learned that oftentimes, as mentioned earlier, what I thought were the solutions to my distress were actually the problem.

I'm in my twenty-sixth year as a therapist, and here's what I've come to believe about people when it comes to change:

1. **People want to change.** No one likes being stuck.
2. For the reasons listed above (and many others I overlooked or outright forgot), **change of any**

kind is hard, even under the best of circumstances. For the purposes of this book, we are talking about changing behaviors. The more obstacles you add, the more difficult it becomes. Good habits and discipline are active ingredients for changing behavior, but they aren't the only ones. Another major ingredient to be addressed when we talk about change is your relationship with the stuff in your head. And by that, I mean your thoughts, feelings, and physical sensations. Hold tight; I'll explain more in upcoming chapters.

3. We often know what we're supposed to do. It may be that **when we start to feel uncomfortable, we hit the brakes**. We're so used to avoiding, delaying, leaving early, or quitting that we don't know what it feels like to continue.

4. People don't change unless the discomfort of staying the same outweighs the discomfort of changing. Again, this is assuming someone is safely make the changes they desire.

The last point clarifies why I stopped treating kids (the age I use to define "kid" somehow keeps going up). Here's how sessions with kids typically went: A well-meaning mom (and I've been this mom) would call about their child who was experiencing "significant anxiety and needed an appointment *this week*."

Parent(s) and the child would come for the first appointment, which is an intake (think "meet and greet"). More times than not, the child was super engaged when telling me about their symptoms. *Finally, someone who understands what's going on and doesn't think I'm crazy. Oh great, I'll have a place I can come and talk about how much I hate my life.*

And then, I got to the point where we'd discuss treatment and what would be involved in that process. If we were going to be working on something the child avoided because it made them anxious, the treatment (vastly distilled) would be intentionally doing that thing over and over until, whether or not they got anxious, they no longer minded; they knew they could ride it out.

But when the kids came to recognize that they'd have between-session work that they'd be expected to do every day? Fuck no, not worth it. Those are ideal kids to work with, actually, because they're honest. What happened more often than not was that parents made the kids come, but the kids weren't doing the work. Or, a kid would say they were interested (and maybe they were, but perhaps they just didn't want to disappoint anyone), but then they didn't do the work.

Until someone's life circumstances get so bad that they're willing to do something about it, long term change isn't likely to happen. As an aside, that's why so many treatments now focus on changing the *parents'* behavior!

Changing just one behavior is, in and of itself, a challenge. So you can, I hope, see why the approach of "slay the whole damn day" by declaring a commitment to lose eighty pounds, reparent your abandoned inner child, and be able to deadlift 350 pounds, all by the end of the quarter, is a recipe for disappointment.

I promised to lay out a variety of mental fitness skills, and you may be wondering where they are. I haven't forgotten; they're coming. But despite how important taking action is and how excited I know you are to get in there and do the damn thing, I want you to first contemplate (remember the contemplation stage of change from earlier in the chapter?) all the reasons to change as well as the reasons not to. I hear a lot of people say, "I *want to want to do it,* but I'm just not up for what it takes." When they say, "what it takes," they are often referring to the investment of time, energy, and attention toward the practice necessary to make change happen. It's okay that this is their perspective. I actually love that kind of radical honesty.

Let's first assess whether you have available space in your mental parking lot for this new task. Right now, think of a change you want to make. Then, take some time to list reasons to make the change on one side of a piece of paper and reasons to stay the same on the other. I want you to be as specific and honest in your responses as possible. We all know a reason to change is "to be happier and not stuck". Don't write down the obvious answers. Challenge yourself to think about what you may have lost (and may continue to lose) as well as who may be impacted by you continuing to stay the same (and who may be impacted by you changing). Make sure to list the facts of what it will require to make this change—whether you see it as a pro or as a con—including actual time to practice or engaging in a good amount of reading, meditating, or even travel time, if that's involved. Remember, there's going to be discomfort in staying the same *and* in changing, so make sure you capture the intricacies of both.

You want your list to be as thorough and thoughtful as possible. I wish I could make the decision for you, but I obviously can't. I can assure you that there will never be a perfect time to embark on making a significant change. That being said, there have been times in my life when I didn't have the necessary bandwidth to make some of the changes I wanted to make. We're human, and in those moments, giving ourselves the grace to come back when we're more able to commit can be the best gift we can give ourselves versus "shoulding" ourselves into action. If you have big events, transitions, or known stressors coming up that will demand your time and attention, it may not be the right time to attempt a significant change. This work is skill-driven behavioral work, and like any new skill, it requires a lot of practice. Sadly, no one gets better at anything by practicing it for only six minutes a day.

WINS

CHAPTER 4

"Don't Think, Just Do."

After the last few chapters, you have a better sense of what's actually involved in making lasting change. You understand that you need a lot more than motivation and inspiration, though both certainly help. When your back is against the wall and you're staring down that pain, you'll need something to help you move *toward* that discomfort instead of back to what's familiar and easier.

That "something" is your "why," sometimes referred to as one's values, goal, North Star, or whatever else is meaningful and impactful in a tough moment. It's the thing that we want to be moving *toward*, but when we're stuck, we're generally inclined to move away from it.

The spirit of the "don't think, just do" mantra—an encouragement to think less and do more—is one I agree with. Too often, we talk ourselves out of doing things, and we cannot change our perception of ourselves without changing our behaviors. That being said, when the challenge is particularly hard, it's helpful to have clarity about what you're moving toward and why before simply taking action. Having that clarity will make it harder to bail on the *doing* when the going gets rough.

The reason having a clear WHY is so important is that you're going to rely on it when you come upon a fork in the road—a moment when you ask yourself, "Do I stay and move forward, or do I go back to where I was before?" That fork in the road is what's referred to as a Choice Point. I wish I had come up with that term, but I didn't. It's based in the principles of Acceptance and Commitment Therapy. A Choice Point is an opportunity to choose behavior that moves you toward your values or desired behavior, or one that moves you away from them. In the most simplistic terms, behavior that aligns with your values/goal/North Star helps move you toward being the person you want to be and, as a result, have a more fulfilling life. In contrast, behavior that doesn't align can move you away from it.

This might sound reductive, but sometimes, we need a really good reason to do hard stuff. I'm guessing you've been in situations where you knew what the right or logical thing to do was, or you knew what you were supposed to do, but it just seemed too much.

Just a little out of your reach. You believe that if only you could get yourself to just do it already, you'd feel so much better.

Everyone's why is different. What's most important is that you figure out yours and keep it front and center. If you're having trouble identifying your why, here are some questions to ask yourself:

- Why is this meaningful to work on?
- What's on the other side if I achieve this?
- How do I want to be remembered?
- How might I feel when I accomplish this?

It can be awfully helpful if we apply this same mindset when we're experiencing distress or discomfort. Ask yourself, "Am I willing to be uncomfortable and continue to do what's important to me?"

You may already be doing this without even realizing it. I recently discovered my gym's VersaClimber class, which is an insanely high-intensity cardio class. I love lifting heavy weights, not doing cardiovascular exercise. In this class, I feel like I'm climbing Mount Everest without oxygen in the middle of summer with no end in sight. And that's just in the first two minutes. A thirty-minute class can feel like hours. Today, as beads of sweat trickled down my face, I asked myself, "Why am I subjecting myself to this?"

Several reasons came to me pretty quickly: it's a good stress reliever, the music is good, it's quick and efficient, and I like the challenge. In broader terms, I endure the discomfort class after class because it serves a bigger purpose—it moves me TOWARD my ideal health and well-being (and possibly a tighter tush).

Just after this realization, it occurred to me that we humans (especially women) are willing to endure lots of things that are super uncomfortable or time-consuming because what's on the other side means enough to us. Think waxing, getting our hair colored every six weeks (which can take hours), radically changing our diets, enduring cosmetic procedures, and giving birth, just to name a few. I'm sure you have some activities coming to your own mind right now.

When we're faced with a challenging experience, we want to focus on actions and behaviors that move us toward what matters instead of behaviors that move us away from what matters. We're used to moving away when we meet discomfort or distress by:

- Avoiding in any form (leaving early, coming late, skipping out, canceling)
- Making up an excuse to yourself or someone else about why you can't do something
- Putting all sorts of conditions into doing something ("I can do it if…")
- Not letting people know how you really feel to avoid a possible conflict (and/or real intimacy)
- Letting it go until the next time

That's just a sampling of ways we "justifiably" avoid doing hard things. Most people are so used to focusing on what they don't like, what could happen, and why they shouldn't do something. Instead, we want to start being intentional about why it matters and what we stand to gain by doing it. If, when you went to the gym, all you focused on was how sweaty and gross you felt, the ache in your muscles, and the shakiness in your arms, you probably wouldn't enjoy working out. If, however, you recategorized all those experiences as signs you were getting stronger and fitter, you might get excited or encouraged because you were moving toward your health and fitness goals.

Here are some other examples of Choice Points people navigate with frequency:

YOU'VE WRITTEN AN IMPORTANT EMAIL

You've read it twice to ensure it's coherent, and you've proofread it for mistakes. But your anxiety about it being perfect won't let you send it. It may occur to you that you'll be seen as a failure if it still has an error. Anxious feelings tell you you should read it again. You do. It looks fine, but those anxious feelings tell you to check it yet again. The cycle repeats, and you become so paralyzed that you cannot send the email.

The moment the anxious thought comes in, you're at a Choice Point. At that point, ask yourself, "Will checking it another time make me any more sure? Can I be confident that this is where it needs to be?"

OUT OF THE BLUE, YOU GET A FUNNY FEELING ABOUT YOUR PARTNER (OR KID, OR FRIEND)

This is your Choice Point.

Do you react to the thought by contacting them to make sure they're all right? Or do you react to the thought by noticing it, and letting it pass, because you are *sure enough* that nothing has changed since this morning?

YOU CHECK YOUR PHONE COMPULSIVELY

Do you check your phone regularly for fear that you'll miss something "important?" Or are you able to put your phone away (and I mean *away*) when you're out with friends?

YOU'RE FOND OF FREQUENT COVID TESTING

Do you immediately take a test (or have a loved one take one) even though you (or they) are asymptomatic and haven't been exposed, just because the possibility is there?

YOU HAVE BACK-UP PLANS FOR YOUR BACK-UP PLANS

Do you have Plans B, C, and D laid out at all times because you need to prepare for any and every possibility?

YOU FREQUENTLY CHECK YOURSELF IN THE MIRROR

Do you need to reassess your appearance every time you pass by a mirror or after every meal to make sure your body hasn't changed?

While these are just a few examples, there are many other types of situations that offer Choice Points, and we each face them all day long. What's most important to consider is: Does the way I'm navigating this Choice Point move me toward or away from my goal (or what matters)?

The more times you can choose to act in ways that align you toward your goal, the better. If you start thinking of Choice Point responses in an all-or-nothing way (all my actions need to be "toward" moves or I've failed!), you're setting yourself up to be disappointed. What you want to be cognizant of is, what's your general pattern? And further, what's the cumulative impact of all this checking/controlling/needing to know for sure? The more you consistently choose behaviors that move you away from your goals, the smaller your life may get and the worse you may feel about yourself. That's why changing things up can be so empowering.

MENTAL FITNESS SKILL #2
Identifying Choice Points

When we're in a sticky situation, it can be really helpful to take some time to identify what "toward" and "away" moves we may be engaging in (or want to engage in). If you can think of a current challenging situation you're experiencing, I encourage you to use that as the basis for this exercise. Otherwise, bring to mind either something that happened recently or a situation where you consistently avoid doing what you want to do or know you should do.

Make two columns, one labeled TOWARD MOVES and the other labeled AWAY MOVES. Begin to list ways you notice you engage in each. Typical "away" moves include procrastinating, scrolling on social media, making excuses, and any other form of avoidance or distraction. Common "toward" moves include asking a friend for accountability, putting a reminder in your phone so you don't forget, doubling up on practicing, going to bed on time, and putting your phone on do not disturb after 9pm.

PRACTICE NOTES

How did you feel doing this exercise? What surprised you?

I hope you're starting to see that the primary moves you need to be making are behavioral. We need to *do* differently, to be more intentional about moving toward what we value.

I know your next question: "What if everything in my head is telling me I can't do it or I shouldn't do it or something awful will happen if I *do* do it. You're telling me to still do it?"

In response, what I will tell you is this: just because something could happen doesn't mean it will. When we get hijacked by our worry, the possibilities somehow become probabilities. That's when we need to slow down, take a step back, and get some distance so we can separate the facts from our stories about the facts. Once we find that tiny bit of space, we can decide what will move us toward our goals and what will move us away from them.

A win can be simply noticing your "toward" and "away" moves. A win can be making the decision to move toward something. A win can be a time when you simply *tried* to move toward something.

WINS

CHAPTER 5

"Choose a Positive Thought."

Perhaps you've heard that in moments of distress, you should simply "choose a positive thought" or "choose happiness."

Here's the issue with that: you cannot *choose* the thoughts that pop into your head. They just…appear. I remember being in one of my lowest moments after being ghosted when someone advised me, with good intentions, to "choose happiness." I wanted to ask how exactly that worked, but I simply smiled instead. Did the fact that I wasn't, in that moment, "choosing happiness" mean I am anti-happiness or anti-gratitude? Absolutely not. I've had a gratitude practice for years. What I'm pushing back against is the belief that you should *only* have positive thoughts and that experiencing certain emotions is so difficult that it should be avoided.

Have you ever believed your thoughts running through your head—only to find out they were completely wrong? Maybe you were convinced you were going to get fired or that someone was mad at you or that you failed at something or that someone didn't like you. In the moment, you would've bet your life that you were right, even if you'd been in that same situation before. You tell yourself, "But this time *felt* different." I've been there too. And, when we believe these thoughts, our behavior reflects that belief. We start worrying, seeking reassurance, replaying conversations, and planning, all around a situation that we've made up and assumed to be true.

The same process happens when we attempt to do things we don't want to do. We react to our distress with assumptions and predictions about how we think it will go. When we're doing or feeling something difficult, it's much easier to slip into believing our assumptions. We don't take a chance because "something *could* happen" turns into "it *will* happen" when that's often not the case.

In order to grow, we need to take some of those chances so that we can see what actually happens when we do the action. Was our prediction correct? Was the reality different? The more experience we get doing this, the more we realize how often our habitual predictions are sabotaging us.

Our perception guides our behavior. And our

perceptions are often wrong. Changing how we think requires repeated new behavior to rewire those pathways. In order to get that process going, you need a way to interact differently with the stuff in your head. By "stuff," I'm referring to your thoughts, feelings, and sensations. Because oftentimes, what's in your head is what's most strongly interfering with your ability to act.

We disengage from the thoughts that sabotage us by intentionally choosing where to place our attention. Simple, but not easy. That's why we call it a practice.

My mom has never been one to give out life advice. She's more than happy to give you her unadulterated, unfiltered opinion, but tangible life lessons are few and far between. The only piece of what I considered advice I can recall receiving from her was when I left for college. She told me to "only date men who drink black coffee, dark beer, scotch, and red wine." Mind you, her husband and best friend of sixty-five years does none of the above, and my ex-husband checked all these boxes. Go figure.

The one piece of advice I *wish* she'd given me was, "Joanna, thoughts are overrated. Most of what goes on in your head are *fakakta* (Yiddish for ridiculous) stories. Don't believe them." That would have been more helpful than the bit about which liquids a fantastic life partner would consume.

To be clear, I'm not suggesting that *all* thoughts are overrated, but many are. Far more, in fact, than we realize.

Thinking about something that exists outside your head is sometimes an incredibly useful pursuit. But in truth, it's actually not thinking that we're doing in those moments; it's problem-solving. It's a process with a starting point (a problem), a middle (thinking), and an end (solution).

Circular thinking (or "looping"), on the other hand, is *not* helpful. I see this a lot when people are excessively worried about their health. It's generally the same pattern. New symptoms, worried thoughts about what it could be, and concern over what horrible treatment they'll have to endure to get rid of it (which creates new worries about missing work, falling behind, and possibly losing their job, which causes more anxious feelings, which makes them feel worse). As in this example, our appraisal of a situation, our ability to navigate a situation, or anything else having to do with the situation may be way off.

I work with many people who have spent an incredible amount of money on therapy, programs, coaches, gadgets, and gear to help them solve a problem or make a change in their life, yet they're struggling more than when they started. Not only are they still struggling to change, but on top of it, they're feeling worse because now they also feel like a hopeless failure (and the debt they may have incurred in their pursuit of the latest, greatest quick-fix doesn't help that feeling). The more cycles of this you experience (attempt to change, struggle to change, quit, feel like a hopeless failure), the harder it becomes to try again, the more you avoid trying, and the more quickly your "hopeless loser/failure" story gets reinforced. This is incredibly unfortunate, because the notion that you can't change simply isn't true.

We all have our stories. The "Oh I can't. I'm not an experienced athlete/gardener/scuba diver/designer" stories. I worked with an incredibly gifted mid-career woman who came to see me because she felt stuck in her life. For years, she had wanted to leave her agency job and go off on her own. Now that her kids were in college, she wanted to take some risks and prioritize herself, but she was held back by her "I'm not someone who makes things happen" story.

Initially, she couldn't imagine applying for grants, holding workshops as an expert, and speaking up in meetings where she was used to deferring to others. We used the framework of imagining what it would be like if she "acted as if she believed she was the expert" (which she clearly was). Were that the case, what would she do? Her answer: she would stand taller, her shoulders back, and she would keep eye contact with others. Instead of only asking questions about whether her opinions were well-received or "good enough," she would state her opinions with conviction.

As a result, with practice, she stopped seeking reassurance from her colleagues that she "was on the right track" and assumed she was, unless she heard otherwise. She started recognizing the pattern that showed up each time she pushed herself out of her comfort zone. That pattern was, she'd tell herself the same story that whatever task she was about to engage in was going to be extremely intense and difficult. Yet once she did it, she realized it often wasn't nearly as bad as she thought it would be. *And,* she realized the payoff was worth it, as colleagues started seeing her as a resource and referrals started coming in.

The more she did, the more she realized she could do, and the less often fear held her back. She now has one of the busiest private practices in our area.

HELPFUL THINGS TO KNOW ABOUT THOUGHTS, THINKING, AND THE BRAIN (IF YOU WANT TO DO HARD SHIT)

JUST BECAUSE YOU THINK IT DOESN'T MAKE IT AUTOMATICALLY TRUE

If you've ever meditated (or tried to), you know that your brain spits up lots of random thoughts. Some can be weird, distressing, and even critical AF. On a "good" day, you may be able to brush off most of these thoughts. But then, there are those days when a thought gets stuck in your head for hours. And since the thought keeps popping up, you mistakenly assume it must be true.

Those full-on stories we continue to tell

ourselves? Because we've been telling them for so long, it can be hard to remember that they may not be true either (or that we've outlived them).

I'm not suggesting that there's never some truth to our thoughts. What I'm suggesting is that we needn't automatically assume that everything we think is true.

When I became a mom, I was woefully unprepared for what was ahead. I was fired from every babysitting job I ever had as a teenager, had never changed a diaper, and my maternal instinct was more for dogs than kids. I was terrified that I would be a terrible mom, and I remember someone older and wiser advising me to aim for being just a "good enough mom."

That term stuck with me and has remained the foundation of my parenting philosophy. But I have certainly struggled, especially when my kids were young, with my ability to be a "good enough" mom. I'd have recurrent thoughts about how I might not be as bonded as I should be, or that the divorce fucked the kids up permanently, or that I wasn't enough of a role model.

When I'm feeling strong and confident, I can let the thoughts pass, but if I'm not having a good day or my kids are struggling, I can lose an hour or more worrying, reassuring myself, seeking reassurance from others, and replaying events trying to figure out—once and for all—if I am good enough. By not keeping my attention in the present moment, my brain replays moments when I messed up, said the wrong thing, made a critical face, was too direct, didn't say "I love you," and forecasted all the ways I could screw them up. Whether I like it or not, any or all of those things may have happened over the years (I'm not sure I entirely trust my memory). The reality is, however, none of my predictions about how much my mess-ups would screw them up have come true.

Having these sorts of intrusive and unproductive thoughts is normal. Thankfully, there is a way to learn to recognize them and reign them in, and it's a practice I work on with clients all the time. I sometimes feel bad that my clients have to suffer through my dog, reality TV, and weightlifting analogies, and I now extend that apology to you as well, but an analogy I use all the time with my clients (and I promised one of them I would put it in the book) when teaching mindfulness awareness is teaching a puppy to heel.

Like Pavlov's dogs, whenever I introduce the concept of mindfulness, my client's say, "Oh, I can't do that." Then, as if on cue (which it essentially is), I launch into my spiel about how our brains are like untrained puppies. As anyone who has ever had a puppy knows that they are full of energy and curiosity. And, as every new dog owner learns, if you give your dog too much leash, chances are you will be dragged around as they sniff piles of shit or other dogs' tushes or roll in dead things. In these moments, do you declare that there's something wrong with your puppy? Would you say that the puppy "can't do walking" or that the puppy is "broken"? I hope not. The puppy is being a puppy! If you want your puppy to heel, you need to choke up on the leash and tell him to "heel." He will still try to pull, at which point you *gently* remind him (over and over) that you want him right next to you. Eventually, he will learn that the word "heel" means that he needs to be right next to you. Consistency, repetition, and patience are key.

The same goes for your mind. Your mind is like an untrained puppy. And, if you're like me and were born anxious, your temperament may be that of a yappy terrier as opposed to a chilled-out mastiff. Regardless of which breed of canine you most resonate with personality-wise, if you give your brain too much leash, it will drag you around—generally to the past or the future. And, since brains do not like uncertainty, they start connecting dots that are not meant to connect in order to reduce the uncertainty. That's how stories are created. Everyone's brain wanders. It doesn't mean you're broken or that anything is wrong with you. If you want your brain to stay in the present, you need to "choke up on the leash" and intentionally return to the present. Like the puppy will keep trying to go back to the as-yet-unexplored bush, your brain will keep trying to go back into the future or the past. You'll have to gently bring it back to the present. *The practice is in the return.*

Does the fact that our brains consistently predict outcomes that never occur mean that we're terrible psychics? Possibly. But what's more likely is that, since brains don't like uncertainty, they will try to figure stuff out and connect that are close by, even if they aren't connected. This is what brains do; they learn by association. To stay out of our stories, it helps to notice when we're getting lost in one and quickly get ourselves back into what's happening in the present moment. That's what it means to put our brains on a shorter leash.

If you start to get lost in your sauce, chances are, you've given your brain too much leash, and you need to shorten it up. The fact that your mind wandered doesn't mean anything other than that your brain is doing brain stuff. It doesn't mean that mindfulness doesn't work for you or that you suck at it. Brain training is like leash training—you engage in gentle corrections, bringing yourself back to the present, over and over again. When you're distressed and feeling intense emotions of any kind, it's very easy to let go of the leash and get lost in thinking traps (or lost in your sauce). In these moments, it can be hard to distinguish between reality and the story in your head. Suddenly you're problem-solving for situations that don't exist, may never happen "but feel so real." That doesn't mean you're "going insane", just highly distressed and need to get back into the present moment.

THERE'S A DIFFERENCE BETWEEN A THOUGHT AND THINKING

According to the Oxford Dictionary, a thought is an idea or an opinion that's suddenly in the mind. *"Peaches are delicious"* is a thought. *"When I get home, I am going to make peach cobbler. Last time I made it was before Covid"* is thinking.

Thinking is a behavior. It's what you *do* with a thought. We cannot control what thoughts show up in our heads, and we may not like many of the thoughts that pop up. But paying attention to the thought by worrying, ruminating, trying to figure it out, working to understand it, attempting to process it, or considering why it showed up in the first place? All of that is *thinking*. And thinking is under our control.

What really helped me learn the difference between a thought and thinking (in any form) was when I started meditating. When I noticed myself lost in thought, I would say to myself "thinking" and gently bring myself back to my breath. If I noticed a thought, I would say "thought" and shift my awareness back to my breath, something I could hear, smell, see, or feel.

When you practice observing, you're reminded that thoughts are fleeting, random, and temporary. The more you practice this observing muscle, especially "in the wild," the more prepared you'll be when things are challenging.

IT'S IMPORTANT TO HAVE GREATER AWARENESS OF THE MEANING WE GIVE TO OUR THOUGHTS

The guy you've been on several dates with doesn't text you back for a day, and your stomach is in knots. The dates have been amazing, the chemistry was off the charts, and he seemed so into you. It felt different from the other guys you've been out with lately, so you're convinced his silence means something happened. Clearly, he's not into you and is already seeing someone else. You're both confused ("I thought he was so into me") and indignant ("Who doesn't text right away?"). You google the appropriate timeframe for returning a text, ask all your friends what they think, stalk his social media to see if he's posted, and cancel your evening plans because you don't feel well enough to go. You spend the evening bummed, telling yourself it's probably over, only to have him text the next night, asking how your day was and wondering when you can get together again.

Sound familiar? If so, we're in this together, as I've done this. More than once.

Think about all the time and energy you wasted on something that wasn't actually happening and the life that passed you by while you were doing so as you asked yourself on repeat, *How did I get here?*

All of this happened, unintentionally of course, because you made an assumption ("He doesn't like me") when he didn't call back in the timeframe you deemed acceptable. When we give something a lot of attention, we send the message to our brains that that "thing" is important. So all that time and energy we spend reacting to our feelings (confused, angry, worried) actually makes the thoughts and feelings stronger, especially since the brain will quickly respond with more of each. As long as you keep giving the situation attention, you're going to keep feeling bummed and continue to engage in counterproductive measures to get rid of it. Albeit unintentionally, you're making those brain pathways stronger. A better plan would be to carry on with your evening plans no matter how you're feeling so you can get out of your head and into life.

INSIGHT CAN BE HIGHLY OVERRATED

I sometimes wonder where we went so wrong in the mental health space, selling people the notion that there's ever "one root cause" of anything. Can anyone give me an example of anything that has only *one* root cause?

Yet that realization doesn't stop people from coming into therapy and wanting—or worse, *needing*—to know the singular root cause of their discomfort before they can take effective action. We've also done people a disservice by telling them their thoughts are so meaningful that they need to be dissected, studied, and then interpreted. Since most thoughts are automatic, this approach seems risky at best and harmful at worst.

The way by which we make meaning of our

thoughts and troublesome thinking patterns can certainly be helpful. However, the conviction that we need to know or understand a thought or thought pattern can be a sneaky way to compel us to justify avoiding taking action. We don't always need to understand or "unpack" our thoughts in order to make a decision. Sometimes all that thinking is what slows us down and keeps us stuck. In those cases, we need to do far less thinking and far more acting.

I once worked with a client whom I'll call Linda. Linda had been working with another therapist for the previous five years and came to me because she was still having trouble making decisions. Regardless of whether the decision had to do with where to vacation or what skillet to buy, she felt compelled to do extensive research. She would have to read all the reviews to find the best option, then find the lowest possible price, then determine the best time to purchase it. Her process was exhausting, and she really wanted to learn how to do it differently. But she also felt compelled to understand *why* she was like this.

Some of the questions she attempted to answer over the course of her initial five years of traditional talk therapy were: Why is it so hard for me to make decisions? What could have happened that would set me up to be like this? How did my parent's divorce when I was eight contribute to my indecision? Is my fear of making the wrong decision a sign I need more parental approval?

Did she get any closer to pulling the trigger faster on decisions during those five years? Nope! Did any of the insights she gleaned translate into behavior change? Nope! I don't think her therapist had any ill intent, nor do I think Linda was intentionally avoiding taking action. But ohmigod, can we please stop doing therapy like this?

If Linda had to make a "quick" decision (in other words, she wasn't allowed to engage in her excessive analytical behaviors), she would feel overwhelmed with worry and uncertainty. The litany of "what if" questions when it came to the idea of making the "wrong"decision plagued her. Our work together focused on how she could feel worried and uncertain *differently* (which you'll learn more about later) while she made a decision. The emphasis was on making a decision, not on how she felt doing it or why she was feeling or thinking a certain way.

THE MORE YOU TRY NOT TO HAVE A THOUGHT, THE MORE YOU'LL HAVE IT

Right now, I want you to imagine a red apple. Imagine how rich its color is, how firm its skin is. Really soak it in—how crispy the first bite would taste, how sweet the juice would be, how refreshing it would be.

Now, for the next minute, *don't* think about the apple. Erase any thoughts of the apple. Ready? Go.

How did you do? If you're like most people, it didn't work. The more you tried to suppress your apple thoughts, the more you had them. Or, if you're the one person who managed to suppress them the whole time (and I know you're out there), chances are, the minute you stopped distracting yourself from them, the thoughts came back.

Trying not to think about something (or feel something) is called thought suppression. I know that most of us are not going around trying to suppress thoughts of fruit, but that may not be the case when the thought or memory is painful or unpleasant.

How many times have you given up sugar and told yourself you can't think about that amazing dessert you want so much? After my husband left, I wanted to erase all thoughts, images, and memories of him because experiencing them was so painful. Yet the more I pushed them down, the more they came back up. This happens a lot when people are going through hard times or feeling stuff they don't want to feel. The process of trying to push thoughts down and having them come back up is called Ironic Process Theory or the White Bear Effect.

Instead of trying to push thoughts away or eliminate them in any way, we want to practice letting them be exactly as they are, whether you like them there or not.

IT'S NOT ABOUT THE CONTENT, IT'S ABOUT THE PROCESS

Content is the specific crap about which we fret.

And content, my friend, is largely irrelevant because content shifts. Process, on the other hand, is how we respond to the situation and where we're going to target our interventions. Your process is far more important. Nowhere is this more apparent than during disagreements with loved ones.

Partner A: It really upset me when you left your stuff all over the kitchen.

Partner B: (looking at his phone) Oh, sorry.

Partner A: (frustrated) I've asked you a hundred times not to and you keep doing it. Clearly you don't care about what I want, because your crap is everywhere.

Partner B: It's just a few things. (annoyed and irritated) Your stuff is out too!

Partner A: (frustrated and angry) Can't you just hear what I say and take care of it?

In this instance, they're fighting about Partner B's stuff being left out (that's the content), but what's more important is how they're fighting. That's their process.

As anyone who's lived with anyone knows, this is neither the first nor last time they will have this argument. Today it's about Partner B's shit being left all over the kitchen. Next week it will be about Partner B not folding the clothes as Partner A asked. The following week it will be that Partner B didn't pack the right clothes for their daughter's field trip as Partner A suggested. And every time, Partner A will be accused of being too controlling, and Partner B will accuse Partner A of not listening or being respectful.

Yes, there are kernels of truth in what both are saying. But you'll never get anywhere if you get bogged down in one person's stuff being left out, the daughter's clothes, or the laundry. It's more useful to focus on *how* they're communicating, *how* they're hearing (or not hearing) what the other is saying, *how* each reacts when they feel "triggered." It's important to recognize that this is their pattern. Content will change, and that's why we don't want to invest too heavily in it. We want to focus on the process of how we interact instead. That's where we can have agency.

I treat a lot of people who are acutely tuned into how their bodies feel and react to perceived shifts and changes. When they first come in, they're in a pattern of avoiding going to an event or otherwise outside the house if they feel slightly "off" for fear that they're getting sick. A typical comment sounds like: "I can't commit to going tonight. I'm feeling off. My stomach hurts a little, and I heard that something's going around my daughter's class, so I don't know if I was exposed to it. I think it's best if I stay close to home." It's entirely focused on content, on what this person is worried about.

When you focus on the content, you get lost in the details and likely try to rationalize your worry or anxiety, searching for certainty where none exists. A process focus, on the other hand, is understanding that when you start "feeling off" or your stomach hurts, you judge those sensations as "bad" or "not how they should be feeling" and then interpret that to mean you could get sick and should stay close to home. Without realizing it, you've labeled the situation as important to your brain, so you're "on guard" moving forward, looking out for more proof that your worry is justified. It's important to understand that if you avoid the activity or event, the worry will only get stronger. Instead, choose to allow yourself to stay in the situation and see if you actually get sick (because in all likelihood, you won't!)!

LET'S REFLECT

What are some of the thoughts/stories that hold you back? If you're having trouble figuring it out, use the prompt "I can't, I'm not a painter/writer/athlete/traveler/etc."

When you think about the change you want to make, what limiting thoughts/stories underlie it?

WHAT'S *YOUR* STORY?

Think of a time when you talked yourself out of doing something and later regretted it. Maybe it was a really cool opportunity that was outside your comfort zone. Or a time you regretted not talking to someone or asking someone out. Or a trip you didn't take because you were worried about all the things that *could* happen (but probably wouldn't). Did you use language like "What if it's too much for me?" or "I can't handle this" or "Maybe something bad will happen"?

Now recall a time when you pushed yourself outside your comfort zone and did more than you thought you could. Maybe you completed an endurance event. Maybe you went to a social event by yourself. Maybe you performed in a recital. How did you talk to yourself then? Did you say things like "I've got this" or "It may not be as bad as I think" or "I'm prepared and ready"? Our self-talk impacts our perception, which impacts what we actually do, the action we take.

MENTAL FITNESS SKILL #3
"Just the facts, ma'am."

This skill is about learning the difference between facts and our interpretation of them. This newfound perspective is such a helpful one to have, especially if you're someone who tends to react to your emotions. I never saw "Dragnet," but apparently the main character was a police detective whose famous line was "Just the facts, ma'am." We're going to use that as the basis for this practice.

I want you to recall a recent situation that got you upset. Then, set your timer for five minutes. First, write down the facts of the situation. What are the objectively true facts? In the next column, list all the assumptions you made about the facts.

For Example:

Facts: The plane was crowded. The person next to me was coughing. There were other people coughing. I was not wearing a mask.

My assumptions: They had Covid. I would get Covid. I would give it to my elderly parents. I would get long Covid and brain fog, causing loss of employment and loss of income, possibly unemployment. I might not be able to support my family.

PRACTICE NOTES

What did you notice? How can you continue to practice (how will you remember to do so)?

WINS

CHAPTER 6

"Life is Too Short for Bad Vibes."

I have nothing against vibes in general. Truth be told, I don't understand what it means to vibrate at a high or low level, but my hairdresser talks about it a lot. She's recommended I listen to music that incorporates a certain vibration in order to attract my jacked empath *and* help with anxiety. As I tell her, if it works for you, great. What I have a problem with, however, is the as-of-late cultural shift toward toxic positivity and the implicit message that distress and discomfort should be avoided. Instead, we should be pushing for allowing and welcoming *all* vibes.

One of the most important skills for quality mental health is learning how to both allow and experience the entire range of human emotions. I suspect most people will read that sentence and not have the slightest clue what it means or where I'm going with it. Stay with me.

When I talk to women, personally or professionally, many comment that they want a partner who is "emotionally available." I also hear this *all* the time on my favorite reality TV show. I don't have the faintest idea what it means, and I'm not convinced many of these women do either, but it sounds good, and I know I've said it too. I've also seen it on countless dating profiles: "I'm emotionally available with no baggage, no drama, looking for the same."

Conceptually, "emotional availability" doesn't make much sense. Think about it. I consider things that are "available" as ready to use or get. A library book is available. Your 10am appointment slot is available. Emotions, however, are mental experiences made up of thoughts, sensations, and urges. They happen automatically, and we cannot control when we feel them. You wouldn't say, "I'm respiratory available" to clarify the fact that you can breathe. Breathing is something you do automatically. It's the same when it comes to experiencing emotions. Therefore, the term "emotionally available" makes no effing sense.

While it doesn't sound as catchy, I'd propose that what we actually need to be (and be looking for) is someone who is emotionally *allowable*. Hypothetically speaking, if you are emotionally *allowable*, which is the state I'd like to encourage you to begin working toward, you:

- Aren't scared of feeling big feelings (that doesn't

have to mean you like feeling them)
- Are able to be responsive in situations versus re-active to your emotions
- May have more meaningful relationships
- Are a better communicator
- May not be avoidant of unpleasant emotions
- Are less likely to avoid hard conversations
- Are less likely to ghost someone
- Are able to set and hold appropriate boundaries (less likely to people-please)
- Ask for what you want and need
- Don't repeat self-destructive or ineffective patterns
- Show up authentically for yourself and others

Most of us did not grow up with any schooling in emotions or feelings. Instead of all those useless dates we had to memorize, it would have been useful to learn some emotion identification, processing, communication, and regulation skills. I honestly thought "fine" and "okay" were feelings until I got to fifth grade and had to pick a feeling from the "How Are You Feeling Today?" sheet. Remember that sheet with all the different faces to represent feelings? Nowhere on there were the options "fine" or "okay."

In order to become emotionally allowable, we have to understand that, regardless of what emotion we're experiencing, it has three components: sensations, cognitions, and urges.

In order to illustrate this, let's use the feeling of anxiety as an example.

When you say, "I'm feeling anxious," you may experience any (or all) of the following **sensations** in your body: knots in your stomach, a lump in your throat, tightness in your chest, tension in your chest, or buzzing in your head. When we talk about sensations, we use words like tightness, lightness, tingling, heaviness. sweating, or racing to describe them.

Cognitions are the thoughts you may experience when you're feeling anxious. Those could sound like, "Ugh, I hate this," "Why is this happening," or "I'm worried I'm going to screw up the presentation." Cognitions are also the labels we slap on our experiences (or those of others). For example, certain stomach sensations become tied to anxiety or dread, and the feeling of "butterflies" becomes tied to fear. Also under the umbrella of cognitions are any memories we may have associated with this feeling, as well as the meaning we make of the feeling.

Urges are the behavioral responses to the emotions. When you feel anxious about giving a presentation to your boss (and your stomach is in knots while you imagine every possible thing that could go wrong), you have the urge to call in sick.

Given what an emotion really is (a combination of sensation, cognition, and urge), you can now fully appreciate why "emotionally unavailable" doesn't make any sense. What I've observed is that if sensations, cognitions, or urges aren't too intense, most people do okay with their emotions or those of the people around them. It's when things get tougher that any of those three components gets stronger or more intense. Let's face it, some emotions feel unpleasant and aversive. And when the emotion you or someone around you is experiencing is unpleasant, aversive, or uncomfortable, all bets are off.

David and Helen called me because they wanted some strategies to "optimize their parenting." Both were highly successful professionals, "problem-solvers extraordinaire," and they wanted to get ahead of any problems they might experience with their nine-year-old. This was a couple who had read every book and bought every gadget, and they talked endlessly about their parenting philosophies because they really wanted to do everything they could to be great parents (their words).

During one of our first sessions, it came to light that their daughter was routinely hitting them, throwing stuff if she didn't get her way, and calling them by their first names despite them not liking it, yet there were no consequences for her behavior. They were concerned that consequences "might break her spirit," and they wanted to encourage her to "express her big feelings." Her big feelings, however, were running them and the entire house. Over time, they decided to try to set some limits. The first (and last) they tried was having her clean up whatever she threw instead of them cleaning up the mess. The first night, she threw all her stuffed animals off her bed, and mom asked her to clean them up. Of course, the child threw more of a fit. This is how mom described her reaction:

"When she escalated, I could feel my blood pressure go up (cognition). My heart was pounding, and I was sweating (sensations). She was screaming at me how much she hated me and how much she wished Daddy was home. I felt so guilty and awful, I wanted to cry. Was this unreasonable? Was it too much? She did have a really hard day and she had a lot of homework. I felt a pit in my stomach (sensation) and thought I could be impacting our relationship for the rest of our lives (cognition). It wasn't worth the risk, so I gave in and told her we could do it together."

When it was Dad's turn to be the enforcer, he had a slightly different experience. When he announced that it was time to get ready for bed, she got predictably upset and threatened to throw all her school stuff (and some of his stuff) off the dining room table. He interpreted this as her being manipulative (cognition) and felt angry. His pulse raced (sensation), his chest tightened (sensation), and his muscles tensed up (sensations). He remembered having thoughts like, "How could a nine-year-old be so manipulative?", "Don't go there with me," and "This is the same shit my mother does" (cognitions and lots of meaning-making). When she didn't stop what she was doing to go to bed, he became more angry (emotion) and noticed urges to yell (urges). He told her again it was time to go to bed, and she ignored him. Every time this happened, he thought, "She has no respect for me" (cognition and meaning-making). This remind-ignore pattern went on until he couldn't hold it in any longer and he blew up.

Interestingly, when they came back to see me, they told me, "Consequences don't work for us." This is not uncommon, but this issue wasn't that consequences didn't work. Between where they were and where they wanted to go were a lot of uncomfortable and unpleasant emotions—in both themselves and their daughter—that they were working hard to avoid. By letting their daughter walk all over them, they never had to face those emotions. If they wanted to see whether consequences *would* work, they'd have to experience distress and allow their daughter to get upset too. Avoiding may work when a kid is young, but the consequences can be graver as she gets older.

Ask yourself how often your behaviors are driven by the situation versus by your feelings? How many times have you woken up and said, "I'm feeling off today, but I'm going to PR (personal record) at the gym, lead a great meeting, and make an amazing dinner tonight!" Probably not often. Me neither. What we're likely to say (and then do) is, "I'm feeling off today so I'm going to skip the gym just in case I'm sick. What if I feel worse and still have to go to this meeting? And I'm not sure about making dinner tonight; maybe I'll order something or just have cereal." Does that sound more familiar?

Many people use how they feel to choose what they do instead of committing to behavior *regardless* of how they feel. It's the difference between "I'll go if I feel up to it" versus "Sure, I'll go." People who generally feel good, capable of handling anything no matter what, don't struggle with this. They don't cancel plans, waffle, struggle with indecision about whether to go, or bail at the last minute. But people at the mercy of their emotions are constantly tracking and checking how they feel, worried about how they might feel, and scared to do things (especially new or hard things) because of how they might feel. We avoid things because of how we feel. This is why being emotionally *allowable* is so important. It doesn't make unpleasant or uncomfortable emotions pleasant, but it demotes them from interminable and terrifying to unpleasant and uncomfortable.

Going back to our example above, using how we feel ("off") to guide our behavior is called emotional reasoning. It's also when we use our feelings as "proof" of something (generally, evidence of the truth) and then use that proof to guide our behavior. It's a common thinking trap in people prone to anxiety and anxiety disorders (and the basis for every reality dating show). *"I know we've only known each other for two days, but I've never had a connection (feeling) like this. Our connection (feeling) is incredible; I get butterflies (sensations) every time I think of you. I've never felt this way. I'm sure you're the one (using feelings to guide behavior)."*

Or, you're talking with your boss (or a co-worker, date, friend, or plumber) and you think you may have overshared about your weekend (feeling unsureness/uncertainty) because you talk a lot when you're nervous (another feeling). Your boss may have given you "a look" as he exited the break room, and now you're convinced (the proof!) that you'll be fired, demoted, or vulnerable to some other catastrophic outcome. You can't stop thinking about it (worried feelings leading to behavior) because the situation feels so urgent and real.

Or, you're back in the workforce after a hiatus and feeling tired and challenged. You might feel inadequate and think the job isn't the right fit for you. Do you assume your feelings are correct and quit by the end of day? Or do you stick it out, assuming your feelings are normal and will pass? Instead of thinking of the options in terms of "right or wrong," consider them in terms of effective or ineffective. If the behavior is part of a pattern, it's more likely to be ineffective. If you stay at the job for another year and it still doesn't feel like a good fit (and you have another offer), it may be an effective time to leave.

When we're triggered, anxious, or upset, we're more likely to relate to our thoughts as if they're real, which makes us more prone to avoid or quit. This can make it harder for us to get from Point A to Point B.

Let's be real, life is full of hard things. If you bought this book, it's likely that you want to do *more* hard things. Or, you notice a gap between where you are and where you want to be. In order to get there, we need to be able to act *in spite of* distress or discomfort. I'm not suggesting engaging in dangerous or risky distress or discomfort, just a bit more than you're comfortable with now. For example, applying for a new job in spite of your fears that you might not be ready, or setting a healthy boundary in spite of feeling uncomfortable doing so, or starting to write your book in spite of feeling worried about whether or not people will like it.

To do that, we need to allow unpleasant and uncomfortable emotions and sensations to move through our body. We need to be emotionally *allowable* in order to be able to do hard things and make changes while feeling a bit of pain—whether physical, emotional, or spiritual.

An important component of becoming distress tolerant is becoming emotionally allowable. Doing that takes practice.

FIVE FACTS ABOUT THOUGHTS THAT HELP YOU BECOME MORE EMOTIONALLY ALLOWABLE

IF LEFT UNATTENDED, FEELINGS ONLY LAST NINETY SECONDS

Shocking, right? The actual chemical process, according to neuroscientist Dr. Jill Bolte Taylor, lasts just ninety seconds. That means the amount of time from the moment the stress hormone is released to the moment it leaves your body is only ninety seconds.

I know exactly what's happening as you read this: your brow is furrowing and you're recalling the last time you felt something unsettling. You're thinking, "That lasted way longer than ninety seconds." Of course it did! As humans, we unintentionally retrigger the circuitry over and over through our behaviors. When we resist, control, analyze, process, figure it out, review, debate, suppress, and avoid, we are sending the message to the brain that this situation is important. That only continues to feed whatever feeling you're feeling. These behaviors become fuel for the fire.

My kids' high school was thirty minutes away, and there's a really hilly part they have to navigate to get there. When they started driving themselves to school, especially in winter, I was a disaster on dark, snowy mornings. The deal was that they had to text me when they arrived. When my oldest and youngest daughters started driving to school, they always texted. My son, however, who is my middle child, always forgot when he started driving himself.

My text (and, eventually, call) was also unanswered because his phone was dead. After thirty minutes or so, he replied to my email that he was fine. I felt increasingly anxious the entire time, which was definitely more than ninety seconds. All the worrying I did and the time spent checking my phone was retriggering the cocktail of stress hormones I was experiencing until I got the email. Without realizing it, we often dig ourselves into a deeper hole.

Once it was my third kid going and my seventh winter doing this, I knew my catastrophic worry thoughts would be there, and I just let them be. I may have had a slight buzz of worry accompanying me as I worked out, replied to emails, and saw clients, but I learned to let that stuff be. Unless I had a real reason to worry (e.g., I heard there was an accident), I assumed all was well until I heard otherwise.

IT'S NOT THE FEELING THAT'S CAUSING YOU SUFFERING, IT'S THE MEANING YOU'RE GIVING TO THE FEELING

Sound familiar? This is the same concept we discussed in chapter 5, when we were talking about thoughts. In my experience, people have a hard time letting their feelings be. I think it's helpful to treat feelings as what they are: an internal experience, like indigestion or gas. What takes the experience of having a feeling from unpleasant to the next level is the meaning we give it.

I'm pretty sure I had emetophobia (intense fear of throwing up) from the ages of thirteen through thirty. I got a terrible case of food poisoning (are there any cases that aren't terrible?) from clams when I was thirteen, and was petrified that it would happen again. I avoided clams, started drinking Coke at even the slightest hint of a sensation in my stomach because my mom told me it was good for stomach aches, kept Pepto Bismol in my purse for years, avoided drinking excessively in case it made me sick, and ran like hell if I was in hearing or viewing distance (or the smell radius) of vomit.

When we traveled, I avoided a huge number of foods I thought might make me sick and, as a result, often didn't eat enough, which of course made me *feel* sick, freaking me out even more. What cured me of this? Vomiting a lot when my kids were young, being around kids who vomit, and being with my ex-husband, who vomited a lot. My son, who's now twenty, inherited his gag reflex and also vomits easily. It's still gross. I don't like it, but my relationship with vomiting has changed.

If my stomach hurts, I don't panic. If I feel sick, I don't do anything except let time pass. All my time and attention aren't spent trying to control whether or not I'm going to get sick. I know that, if it happens, it'll suck. And also, I'll cope.

THE MORE YOU TRY TO CONTROL YOUR FEEL-INGS, THE MORE THEY'RE GOING TO PERSIST (AND GET STRONGER)

As mentioned, we are not always in control of how we feel, nor are we meant to only feel happy. We are meant to experience a big range of feelings, some pleasant and some unpleasant. I get it that the unpleasant ones don't feel good, but we screw ourselves any time we start trying to control them (more on this in the next chapter).

My client, Janet, had just separated from her partner of fifteen years, and her friends wanted to do something special, so they planned a girls weekend. Janet loved getting pampered, so they went to a spa where they could hike and get massages. Janet was so moved at how thoughtful a gesture it was. Her friends declared the weekend "GVO" (Good Vibes Only). It was to be about "laughter, love, and leaving the past behind" (as if that were even possible).

They had lovely intentions but ignored the reality that Janet *also* felt sad, worried, and exhausted. Yet she felt like she couldn't express those feelings because they weren't GVO, and they'd bring down the vibe. So she stuffed them down until she couldn't anymore, when, seemingly out of nowhere, she got more emotional and her fuse got shorter until she melted down into a panic attack followed by a "spectacular ugly cry" (her words) in the hot tub. While her friends were acting from a place of love, forcing positivity made her feel worse and amplified her distress.

"NAME IT TO TAME IT" REALLY DOES WORK

Dan Siegel, MD, came up with the phrase "You have to name it to tame it" to describe the practice of labeling your emotions. It's also called "affect labeling," and it can help you identify, regulate, and detach from strong emotions.

Here's how it looks: You notice a mole on your back, and your first thought is, "What if that's skin cancer?" Before you know it, you're mining memories, trying to figure out how long it's been there, contorting your body to inspect it. You may have diagnosed it at Stage 4 (despite having no medical degree), and you're worrying about what the treatment will be. Your stomach is in knots (sensations), you have a lump in your throat (sensations), and this is all before you even start searching Google (urge).

In this situation, I generally hear people say, "I'm freaked out (anxious)" and then some iteration of "I have cancer." Whenever someone tells me "I'm anxious," I remind them that they do not have a name tag clarifying that their name is Anxious. I remind them that they are simply *feeling* anxious.

Anxious is a temporary feeling, and putting the phrase "I am feeling" in front of it creates some distance between you and the feeling. To put distance between someone and the thought "I have cancer," one could say, "I'm having the thought I have cancer" or "I'm aware I'm thinking I have cancer." The process of putting distance between you and your internal experience is called cognitive defusion. When any two things are fused together, there's no space between them. That's great if we're talking about steel beams on a building, but not so great if thoughts are fused in our heads, limiting our ability to respond flexibly. By creating space, you give yourself the opportunity to respond differently. This famous quote, often attributed to Victor Frankl, fits well:

"Between stimulus and response lies a space. In that space lies our freedom and power to choose a response. In our response lies our growth and our happiness."

YOU CAN TREAT EMOTIONS LIKE WAVES

I find it helpful to think of emotions as waves (this is not an original idea, by the way). Some are big; some are small; some are intense; some are not; sometimes they come often because there's a storm; sometimes there are no obvious waves, and the water is still like glass. But regardless of external circumstances (like weather), waves are always moving.

Like waves, emotions build, peak, and then pass. Most of us only notice the wave when we're at the top of it. We also don't believe we ever come down because it can feel like you're panicky *all day*, worrying for *hours,* crying for *days.* But no emotion truly lasts that long—unless we retrigger the circuit. So what's more than likely happening when you feel like an emotion is sticking with you for hours or days is that you're retriggering the circuit, and only noticing when you're at the top of the wave.

I've already outed myself by admitting that this stuff is still quite hard for me when my kids are involved. I can manage my own distress much better than I can manage situations when my kids are upset. My eldest was in college during Covid-19, and her school took Covid precautions really seriously. The first time she got Covid (in December 2020), she had to quarantine in a hotel room way off campus and was instructed to stay in her room all day. The hotel was in a very run-down part of the city, she wasn't allowed to accept food delivery, and taking a walk outside wasn't permissible (which made absolutely no sense). The school delivered a brown-bag meal twice a day, which they left outside her door as if she was in prison. She *felt* like she was in prison. This was the protocol for ten days.

As my daughter's mental health started declining from the isolation (on day three), I started losing it (in other words, climbing the wave). I was worrying myself sick that she was getting more depressed. I asked her siblings excessively how they thought she seemed, emailed school personnel, and googled to see how contagious she likely was. These were all unproductive behaviors that kept me at or near the top of the wave. By day six, I was mentally exhausted and of no help to her. I realized I had to stop trying to control the outcome (swimming against the wave) and work on myself.

I knew all my worry and anxiety weren't going anywhere, but instead of focusing on them, I committed to engaging with my normal routine. I stopped trying to feel better about the situation and not feel so worried. I accepted whatever I was feeling because it was there, whether I liked it or not. When I got an urge to seek reassurance, google something, or check in with her for the umpteenth time, I set a timer to delay engaging. When I was really worked up, I would remind myself of the ninety-second rule and set my timer for two minutes. For those two minutes, I would go and do something *while* I felt whatever I was feeling. I knew I could feel anything for two minutes; I've given birth three times.

I would cook while I felt anxious, and I would walk the dog while I felt unsure. I could live life *while* I felt those feelings, without doing anything to make them stop. And, when the two minutes were up, I would do another two minutes. And on and on until my urge passed. The timer held me accountable to letting that stuff be. You're not trying to let it *go*. That implies it shouldn't be there. You're only trying to let it *be* and get better at feeling however you are feeling in that very moment.

We'll talk more about letting it be in chapter 9 because it's a critical behavior to practice. Every step you take toward letting your feelings *be* rather than shaming yourself for not being able to let them *go* significantly strengthens your distress tolerance muscle.

MENTAL FITNESS SKILL #4
Learn to Ride the Wave

Rationale for the skill: As Jon Kabat-Zinn famously stated when describing mindfulness, "You can't stop the waves but you can learn how to surf." That's what we are learning to do with this one. When we're feeling an unpleasant or uncomfortable emotion or sensation, we want to let it *be*. The less we do, the better. When we're in doing mode, we're swimming against the waves. When we're in an allowing mindset, we're riding it.

Dr. Alan Marlatt, a psychologist and researcher in substance use, coined the term "urge surfing" in the '80s to describe riding out the urge to use drugs or alcohol. He recognized that keeping people in the present moment (versus lost in their stories) helped enormously, and people learned that their urge was temporary and passed. The skill is to learn to let the urge peak and pass on its own. The less attention we give it, the faster it will pass.

If you don't want to feel like you're controlled by the shit in your head, this next exercise is for you. Yes, it's hard, but so are many aspects of life!

Exercise: Set your timer for five minutes and just be. Choose a position and commit to it. Commit to not checking your phone, not itching itches, not moving, not thinking. I want you to get uncomfortable. I want you to get itchy, bored, frustrated, and impatient. I want your mind to wander (that is what brains do). Your job during this time is twofold:

- Don't engage with any discomfort or distress that comes up.
- Choose where to put your attention. Every time your brain wanders, and it will, gently bring it back to your anchor. Your anchor can be anything happening with your five senses. Do the same when you start judging your performance or the purpose of the exercise. Just notice and gently bring yourself back to your anchor.

PRACTICE NOTES

What was your experience like? Did anything surprise you? What was the most challenging part? What did you learn about your ability to allow and accept your thoughts, feelings, and sensations for those five minutes? What will you tweak the next time you practice this exercise?

WINS

CHAPTER 7

"It's Wine O'Clock Somewhere."

This particular piece of word art always makes me shake my head. I haven't seen anything in the scientific literature about it just yet, but I hear a lot about "women and their wine." I've even heard it referred to as "mommy wine culture" in popular media. Like most things in life, there's nothing wrong with wine. If, however, your go-to way of coping with distress or discomfort is your glass of rosé, I'd read on.

Yes, we tend to resist stuff that's unpleasant and uncomfortable. Of course we do. Who wants to feel bad? And, as mentioned in chapter 2, many of our justified solutions to distress and discomfort end up becoming newfound problems.

It's precisely what the saying "It's wine o'clock somewhere" is speaking to—how we cope (or, more to the point, escape) the discomfort or distress we're feeling.

I had a client who desperately wanted a romantic partner. She was in her early thirties, highly educated, very successful, quick-witted, and an amazing cook. On the surface, it looked like she had it all, except she had never had a relationship last longer than eight months, and she really wanted to get married and have kids. She didn't identify as being anxious. She just, as she put it, "liked to be in control and didn't like uncertainty. You know, a typical type-A personality."

Dating was quite hard for her since she "didn't want to waste her time with losers" (again, her words), so she'd grill dates about their past relationships, financial situation, and baby timeline—all within the first month. If she didn't hear from them after a day or so, she'd text them to "check in," and she had to know all details of dates and plans because she "didn't like surprises." Relationships didn't last, and she was concerned that she was too much of a control freak to have a relationship. She wasn't broken (or any kind of freak). She was resisting the discomfort that came from not knowing the details of how things would play out. She was highly anxious and used controlling behaviors (which this chapter is all about) to manage or outright rid herself of distress.

Once we explored this some more, she was able to recognize a cycle she'd unintentionally been in since childhood: When she felt any hint of uncertainty, she would do something to make it go away. When her stomach felt off, she would immediately go to the nurse. When she was worried she wouldn't do well on something, she would study more. When she worried she wouldn't get into an Ivy League school, she would take thirty practice tests before the ACT. When she worried she wouldn't get a good internship, she stayed in on weekends to do interview preparation and make spreadsheets that detailed her options. Dating and relationships were especially hard for her since she couldn't control the outcome, and that made her feel unsettled, uncertain, and uncomfortable.

Remember, most of us did not grow up learning how to feel our feelings. This is how the cycle goes for most people: They experience a thought/memory, then they judge it as bad or incongruous with how they see themselves ("I'm not a _____"). Then, they feel anxious or some other unpleasant emotion, and then they react in order to get rid of the feeling.

In Acceptance and Commitment Therapy, we call this experiential avoidance. It's an "unwillingness to remain in contact with distressing internal experiences along with the attempts to control or avoid distressing internal experiences."

HOW THE DOMINOES FALL

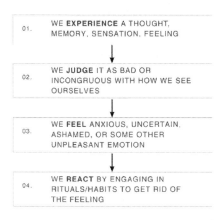

01.	WE **EXPERIENCE** A THOUGHT, MEMORY, SENSATION, FEELING
02.	WE **JUDGE** IT AS BAD OR INCONGRUOUS WITH HOW WE SEE OURSELVES
03.	WE **FEEL** ANXIOUS, UNCERTAIN, ASHAMED, OR SOME OTHER UNPLEASANT EMOTION
04.	WE **REACT** BY ENGAGING IN RITUALS/HABITS TO GET RID OF THE FEELING

Without any knowledge of how to do it differently, we react instinctively to make the unpleasant feelings stop. Something doesn't feel good? Avoid it or do something to make it stop. Makes sense, but as you've learned, the more you try not to have a thought/feeling/emotion/sensation, the more you're going to have it and the stronger it's going to be. And, by avoiding something, you're likely moving away from what's important to you in the longer term. The avoidance offers short-term relief, but in the long term, it's moving us away from what we want. We trade a hit of short-term comfort for longer-term freedom. By avoiding our internal experience, we unintentionally make our distress stronger and limit our behaviors. Remember from chapter 4, we want to be moving *toward* our goals, not away from them.

You're probably wondering what these resistance behaviors look like, so I've lumped them into broad categories. See if any feel familiar to you. And before you get pissed at me for listing exercise or acquiring a beautiful crystal as an avoidance behavior, here's the fine print: None of these behaviors are, in and of themselves, good or bad. That would be too easy.

When you identify a behavior that makes you go *hmmm*, here are the nuances to consider:

- How often do I use this? (one-off or repeatedly)
- How reliant am I to use/have it? ("Just in case" counts)
- Is doing it moving me toward or away from what I want (and at what cost)?

RESISTANCE BEHAVIOR TYPES

AVOIDERS AND PEOPLE-PLEASERS

These are people who, when confronted with distress or discomfort, want to avoid, distract themselves, or leave early. Or, they'll go, but with lots of safety behaviors "just in case" or "to be safe." Alternately, this resistance behavior can show up interpersonally through people-pleasing: "I'm fine(ing)," shutting down, disconnecting, deflecting or projecting. In short, when the heat is on, avoiders and people-pleasers avoid.

I know a lot of people who like to have Xanax (or a drug like it) with them "just in case" they get really anxious. My dad is one of these people when he travels. He says it makes him feel better to know it's there in case he gets "wound up." I've never seen him take it (even though we beg him to), but he feels safer if it's there.

CROWDSOURCERS/REASSURANCE-SEEKERS

These are the people who have trouble making decisions, question themselves, always like to get second (through millionth) opinions "just to be sure." It doesn't matter that they don't know what they're talking about (or the person they're talking to). They'll still ask.

COMFORT ZONERS

These are people who are weighed down by inertia, for whom the pain of staying the same has not yet outweighed the pain of change. These people are stuck in their comfort zone, even if they say they want change. There's little or not enough discomfort to incite change. I know a lot of people who would rather stay stuck (unintentionally) than risk doing something new and possibly "failing."

Whether it's staying in the same job versus going out on your own, setting a limit with your kids, not dating, or buying another self-help program but only committing halfway, if there are no consequences to staying the same, why change? People in this category avoid distress by staying stuck.

NUMB-OUTERS

When people in this category start to feel uncomfortable or distressed, they want to shut it down by self-medicating or otherwise numbing out. Behaviors include (but are not limited to) all the things we use to numb or neutralize how we feel. That could involve booze, shopping, substances, food, porn, exercise, not eating, sleeping, shopping, working, watching TV, or scrolling social media.

At least once a week, someone will justify this behavior to me by saying they have "an addictive personality." An "addictive personality" is not a clinical term, but still, it's used as if it were a real diagnosis (or a real thing). Functionally, I think that having an "addictive personality" refers to someone who uses something compulsively to regulate their internal discomfort. That's the learned part of a behavior. If you have genetic or environmental vulnerabilities toward addiction, your predisposition for use and misuse of behaviors that help you numb out probably increases.

DUMBO'S FEATHER HOLDERS

People in this category use mantras, weighted blankets, crystals, oils, supplements, or anything similar to feel better and control distress. I have nothing against any of these mechanisms, and I've dabbled in all of the above when trying to get rid of a feeling. Yet, while I smelled amazing from dousing myself with the oils, I was still an anxious mess—just an anxious mess weighed down with crystals. A key indicator was that I wasn't appreciating my crystal for its beauty as I was anxious. I wanted it to *make me feel better now!* There's a difference.

Had my anxiety dropped as I was holding my crystal, I could have made the false connection that I needed my crystal to calm down. I could have determined that the crystal somehow had magical properties, like Dumbo's feather, that helped me calm down versus recognizing that all emotions naturally come down and pass on their own. Just as Dumbo didn't think he could fly without his feather, one could start believing she can't go places or do things without her safe objects (consider how many people can't go places without their water bottles!). When we become convinced that it's the gizmo that's responsible for the relief, we become reliant on it and lose confidence in the fact that we don't have to *do* (or buy) anything to find relief.

PROCRASTINATORS

These are the people who, when they start to feel uncomfortable or distressed when they have to do something, distract themselves with another activity. Instead of feeling the distress or discomfort of getting started, it can be easier (in the short term) to organize your shit for the hundredth time or wait until you're more inspired or your space is perfect. The excuses are as infinite as your imagination.

COMPULSIVE SELF-HELPERS

These are people who, at the first sign of discomfort or distress, turn to their favorite podcaster, influencer, writer, guru, or fitness instructor to try to get rid of the feeling (or "negativity"). There's nothing wrong with getting hyped up or getting some inspiration, but I've seen a lot of people at best spin their wheels and at worst spend tens of thousands of dollars going to workshops, enrolling in masterminds, and buying self-help book after self-help book to find their inner warrior, lean into their feminine energy, or get more hyped. The problem is, they don't know how to translate any of it into actionable steps. And ninety-nine percent of the time, they're chasing a feeling (outcome), but still feel ill-equipped when life is inevitably difficult.

GOOD VIBES ONLY/NO NEGATIVITY FOLKS

This is the person who is all about positivity, all the time. Remember Janet's friends who took her on a trip to distract her from her separation and had a Good Vibes Only rule for the weekend? This is that, but all the time, not just for a weekend.

I'm all for feeling good, but there's an implicit belief that "feeling bad" should be controlled, managed, and "fixed" right away. There's no room in this person's experience for feeling anything but "good" feelings. If they start to struggle, they work harder to suppress their feelings until they either implode or explode.

OPTIMIZERS

These are the people who try to avoid ever being uncomfortable or distressed by optimizing every aspect of their life. They can be highly regimented around their sleep, diet, stress, exercise, fluid intake, supplements, screen time, and hormones to try and maximize everything. Spontaneity and flexibility are not their strong suits, because either of those would disrupt their routines.

MICROMANAGERS (CONTROLLING BEHAVIORS)

Caveat: I am not talking about the kinds of controlling behaviors we see in abusive relationships. I am talking about behaviors like micromanaging partners, kids, employees, and one's image in order to try and reduce any chance of something going wrong.

Another example is trying to control the "art" of finding the optimal partner—so much so that they never get into a committed relationship. That can contribute to someone being both emotionally unallowable and avoidant.

Have you ever known a person who seems really lovely but is impossible to get to know? Every time you see her, the conversation stays purely topical, and if you try to get deeper, she steers it right back to the surface? She seems guarded, as though she's managing her image?

Oftentimes, these people are highly anxious, terrified of being rejected, embarrassed, or afraid of being judged in a negative way. They'll try to mitigate the distress by controlling their conversations, what people know about them, and how much they say. A metaphor I often use with my clients to describe this resistance behavior category is a realtor who is trying to sell a beautiful home but only letting people into one room.

WISHFUL THINKERS

I could have lumped this one under Avoiders or Numb-Outers, but I think this title is catchy for the daydreamers and "I wish-ers." If your reality is difficult, and you're feeling a lot of pain, it can be appealing to start daydreaming about a time when life was easier or an idealized situation you wish you were living. If this happens once, it's not a big deal, but it becomes a coping mechanism for a lot of people when faced with a challenge.

Your present doesn't have to be painful to have wishful thinking. The feelings of boring, consistent, and stable can also be uncomfortable enough for some people to begin engaging in wishful thinking.

I had a client, Paul, who was in his early forties. He was married to his college sweetheart, and they had three young kids. He had a good job, a solid relationship, and a wide peer network, but he felt unsettled in

his life. Whenever he felt "the void," he would remi-
nisce (in his head) about his college years. He would
replay old memories on a loop, and his refrain was, "If
I could just get back to the feeling I had then, I could
be happy." He compared every experience he had to
those years, and he compared every feeling he felt in
the present to the way he imagined feeling decades
ago. He was driving himself and everyone around him
crazy because he wouldn't stop trying to live in the
past.

FOR REFLECTION

As you read those categories, where did you see
yourself? Did anything surprise you? Did you notice
any strong feelings come up around any of them, perhaps an area to come back to when you have some distance and clarity?

In the short term, these resisting behaviors work.
In the longer term, however, they can become problematic. They provide momentary relief (the principle
of negative reinforcement), and that's why we use
them. But the more you do something, the more reliant
you may become on it, and that can have consequences.

If you have a genetic predisposition toward substance misuse, eating disorders, anxiety disorders, or
depressive disorders, repeated use can become

problematic. If you're consistently looking to others for reassurance or to help you with decision making, you're losing opportunities to build autonomy and confidence. And if you're spending more time trying to undo the past or tripping about some future event, you're robbing yourself of the chance to be in the present, connected to whatever is happening now and seeing what actually happens in future moments.

So, now that you know all the various ways you resist unpleasant feelings, what do you do *instead*?

The key to being able to move through unpleasant feelings and no longer allowing them to stop you from doing the things you want to do is to consciously *experience* them. What I mean by this is, you ride them out, allowing them to be there without trying to make them go away. You let them be. You stop doing something based on how you feel and start simply allowing how you feel. You do nothing with the stuff in your head while going on with life. Rather than letting the distress prevent you from doing hard things, you practice allowing the distress to be there as you do those things. In this way, you begin to do distress and discomfort differently.

Let's say you're nervous about going to a party post-Covid. Perhaps you have an older person living in your home with you or you're working through general nervous feelings around your own health. Your thoughts center around the familiar "what if" questions: "What if it rains, and we hang out indoors?"

"What if there are a lot of people?" "What if so-and-so isn't wearing a mask?"

The more you think, the more anxious you become. You then try to stop that anxiety, obviously, because it's uncomfortable. You may find yourself making contingency plans for every possible situation that could arise, checking the weather and asking your friends for reassurance.

All of these behaviors are like pouring gas on a fire. The more you try to solve the discomfort, figure it out, or gain certainty, the more anxious you become and the deeper the hole you dig. It's exhausting—and completely ineffective.

What I'm suggesting that you do instead is, acknowledge your initial, unpleasant feelings. Using the party example, acknowledge that you're anxious about going. Then, practice being uncertain and uncomfortable by not engaging in all the behaviors to feel better, while still attending the party.

The brain learns what we show it by our actions or inactions. If we consistently show it that we can experience uncomfortable thoughts and feelings, over time the brain becomes less sensitized to the trigger. The key is to let those feelings come and go without engaging with them or trying to solve/numb them. We show the brain over and over by our actions that the situation is not a true threat.

This takes time. The more you do it, the more you learn you can do it (even if you're anxious while doing it). You'll continue to build confidence during the process. Every time you feel anxious, look at it as an opportunity to practice feeling the thoughts and uncomfortable feelings while you're living life. Simply acknowledge, "Oh, I'm feeling anxious. This is uncomfortable, and I'm going to continue on with my day."

By now, I hope you better understand the scope of distressing feelings and sensations as well as what distress tolerance and intolerance are and are starting to see why this concept is so important when it comes to unhooking for your stories, getting out of your own way, and doing hard things. More importantly, how it may be interfering with your ability to stick with the hard things you've committed to.

You also understand why what you've been doing (trying to get rid of your distress and discomfort) doesn't work in the long run. If your memory is waning like my own, here's your reminder: what you resist, persists. And, in order to actually do hard things (or get comfortable being uncomfortable or do one thing a day that scares you), you're going to have to act in spite of your perception that you can't. Before we jump to further action, it's important for you to get clearer about where distress intolerance may show up for you.

I gave you some examples in chapter 2, but here are some more, just in case:

- I hate feeling this way; I'm going to take a Xanax to chill.

- My stomach shouldn't be in knots; let me google what this could be.
- I hate waiting to see if he'll call, so I'll text him to remind him I'm still alive.
- Ugh, this feeling makes me crawl out of my skin; get me out of here.
- I'm worried I blew the interview. Let me crowdsource this and see what my friends and family think.
- I don't want to tell Joanna I have a girlfriend, so I'll ghost her.
- I don't want to own my mistakes, so I'll blame them on someone else.
- I'm scared my friend will be disappointed if I don't go, so I'll go.
- I don't like silence, so I always fill it.
- If I have an itch, I must scratch it.
- If I have a thought I don't like, I can't let it go.
- If I'm going to have sex, I need to be liquored up. I'm too self-conscious otherwise.
- I "have anxiety" so I rub my crystals (or use my oils) to try and make it go away.
- I don't like conflict, so I'll do whatever makes you happy.
- I don't like saying no, so let me tell you exactly why I can't do it.

RECOGNIZING THE TIPPING POINT

You know the point right before you decide to

quit something hard? We're going to call that point the tipping point, and most people quit right before they hit it. It's kind of like the adage "three feet from gold" (where the guy has dug a 347-foot hole looking for gold, but then quits when he's just three feet from the treasure he seeks. The moment when he quits is his "tipping point").

You may not always be aware of your own personal tipping point, or you may hit it so automatically and so often that you've forgotten that whether or not you hit it is actually a choice. In either case, the more often you hit it, the lower your threshold for distress and discomfort gets. That only serves to make your world smaller (and this happens gradually, which is why we often don't notice it's happening or has happened). We're going to call that "lowering the tipping point." When you do that, not only does your world become smaller, but so does your perception, belief, and trust in yourself. Over time, things you used to do become harder or even avoided completely. When you do things that are outside of your comfort zone and build your tolerance for distress and discomfort, that moves your tipping point upward.

The good news is that your tipping point is not fixed. In order to raise it, you need to start doing distress (or whatever feeling you're resisting) differently. And, to do that, you need to find those situations—situations that either exist only in your head or actual situations you can see—that evoke those internal experiences. As the popular quote says, "It's not about the situation, it's about your reaction to the situation" that matters.

Nowhere is this more obvious than in interactions with people. As experienced as I am as a therapist, I am a terrible couples therapist. Being a good one is a skill and an art. Earlier in my career, I would work with couples and a familiar dynamic presented itself:

Person A: "If only you did X, then I would do Y." "If you stopped X, I wouldn't do Y." (Parents do this too.)

Inevitably, the person projecting the blame, who was intolerant of their and everyone else's discomfort, really believed the problem lay outside of them. I'm not suggesting that the other person did not have a piece of responsibility. But what the speaker didn't appreciate was that it wasn't about the other person or the situation. It was about *how* they were interacting with the other person. And that was driven by their internal experience.

MENTAL FITNESS SKILL #5
How I Resist

When I think about avoidance behaviors, a.k.a. "control strategies," I think about the Baskin Robbins marketing strategy of having thirty-one flavors of ice cream every month; it allows for a different flavor of the day, every day. You may have a favorite way to avoid, *and* that way can change at any time. Your job, therefore, is to start building capacity to spot those avoidance tactics.

Toward that end, I want you to pick one weekday and one weekend day to do some self-monitoring. Self-monitoring is an incredibly useful tool—*if* it's done in the moment. It is not useful if you try to log your day from memory at 10pm. Research supports this.

I want you to log:

- Time of day
- Situation you avoided/wanted to avoid or emotion/thought/sensation you wanted to avoid
- Avoidance/resistance category (feel free to use categories given above)
- Level of distress (ranked 1-10, with 10 being the highest)
- Feeling and/or sensation you were resisting

PRACTICE NOTES

Did anything surprise you? Extra credit: How might you use riding the wave or urge surfing when you bump up against one of these situations in the future?

MENTAL FITNESS SKILL #6
Identifying the Target

The "target," in this case, is the point of where

you're gripping. Before we can work on getting more tolerant, we need to identify precisely where you're most distress *in*tolerant. There are several ways to identify these areas:

Remember, the two components of distress (in)tolerance are perception and behavior. What situations do you preface with "I can't bear to…" (or "I can't handle…" or "It's too much to…") so I don't [insert activity]." When women learn I am a powerlifter, they often say, "I would love to be able to do that, but that's too hard for me." Or, a trainer tells women to do push-ups, at which point they immediately go to their knees and say, "I can't do real ones, that's too much for me" without even trying.

Think of a change you really want to make, and consider what gets in the way. Not the logistical challenges, but the thoughts, feelings, and sensations that might make change hard. For instance, perhaps you really want to be a better parent/partner, and you know that means *not* problem-solving for the other person. When they're distressed, you feel distressed and start executing on their behalf, even though you know it's the wrong thing to do.

Refer back to your self-monitoring log—the list of situations or feelings you avoid (or want to avoid) that you identified in Mental Fitness Skill #5. For instance, you find that you struggle feeling bored, so you mindlessly scroll on your phone instead of feeling the feeling of "bored."

Awareness is always the first step. What you're creating here is awareness of the areas where you're being distress intolerant. In the next chapter, you'll learn another tool for treating those situations differently—how to allow the distress instead of resisting it.

WINS

CHAPTER 8

"Get Out of Your Head."

Have you ever described a movie, show, or book as "gripping?" What does that word mean to you? To me, it means I'm locked in with my full attention, my senses are engaged, my stomach may be in knots, my heart may feel like it's racing, and I'm still thinking about the situation after it's over. Not to split hairs, but technically, movies don't grip us, we grip them. *It's our engagement with them that creates this experience.*

The phrase "get out of your head" is one I support. I WANT you to get out of your head—but the challenge with this statement is that people have no idea where to go (and how to stay there).

Think of all the attention, in any number of forms, we may give to the movie. We replay scenes in our heads, read about the film, discuss it with friends, think about it, or watch trailers. Just as we can grip a good piece of art, we can also grip our thoughts, feelings, and sensations, especially if we don't like them. All the mental machinations—let alone behavioral ones—we do when we feel discomfort or distress is "gripping." Another way to think of it is zooming in on the discomfort or distress.

Other ways we do this:

- Asking your partner (or perhaps instead your kids/friends/family/boss) for the nth time if they think you're okay
- Visiting just a few more websites (in addition to the few you already visited) to be sure you really understand something or are making the best choice
- Replaying that conversation with your boss yet again because it felt awkward
- Crowdsourcing opinions on your date's text to get others' take on it
- Asking Dr. Google every time something feels off in your body
- Trying to figure out if the feelings you're feeling are a sign from the universe (your intuition)

Intuitively, we think that if we could just figure it out or get the information we want, we'd feel better. But ninety-nine percent of the time, we find the loophole or the "yes, but…" and still need more.

Right after I was ghosted, I was tied up in knots, the muscles in my neck, shoulders, and jaw gripping. My hands were perpetually in fists, and my breath was shallow and rapid. I had a running mental reminder to relax these areas, but I was also gripping my thoughts about why he ghosted me and all the clues I may have missed. ("Did he really have Covid? Were his kids really sick when he canceled that date? Was it a sign that 'Catfish' and 'Dr. Phil' were his favorite shows? What if something happened; he did mention all these medical tests. Were those all lies too? Was he ever truthful, or was it all lies? If I got this duped, am I qualified to be a therapist?) It felt like my mind was filled with both rabbit holes and landmines.

In most of the above examples, uncertainty is the main through-line. But distress isn't limited to uncertainty. According to the Oxford Dictionary, distress is "extreme sorrow, anxiety, or pain." All of those fall under the "feelings that suck" umbrella. That's not a clinical term, nor is it non-judgmental, but it is accurate. To be fair, there are a lot of other emotions that fall under this umbrella as well, so it can be helpful to think of them in four broad categories, according to the Centre for Clinical Interventions' handout on distress tolerance:

Sad feelings: this group includes feelings along the sadness continuum (with varying ranges of intensity).

Feelings such as grief, despair, hurt, shame, sadness, depression, embarrassment, vulnerability, misery, and disappointment.

Mad feelings: This group includes, but is not limited to, feelings such as rage, annoyance, frustration, bothered, irritated, agitated, jealous, disgusted, and hatred.

Scared feelings: This group includes, but is not limited to, feelings such as uncertain, confused, unsure, nervous, worried, panicked, bothered, dread, fear, and terror.

"Just not right" feelings: This is an important and often overlooked group. This is the feeling or sensation that something's not right or not "just so." You feel "off" and that feels intolerable or uncomfortable. You see this a lot with people who have extra-sensory nervous systems. Think of your friend who can't walk into a room without straightening your shit or fluffing your pillows because they "just can't relax until it's straightened up."

As much as some will try, we cannot escape distressing feelings. The situations that evoke them may be unpleasant and painful or even boring, and the sensations that come with them are uncomfortable. Some might even say it physically hurts to feel distressed. Or, they may confuse feeling sick or, in the extreme, dying (or having a cardiac event) with intense states of distress.

When we experience something we don't like, the thinking machine starts going and we start creating stories: "This feeling will never end." "My life will never get better." "This always happens to me." "This sucks." "Everybody's life is so much better than mine." "Why do I have the worst luck?" "I think I'm cursed." You get my drift. We end up taking an already shitty situation and making it even shittier.

The prevailing wisdom has always been: if you feel bad, do what you can to feel better (e.g., get rid of this feeling *right now*). If you're actually in danger, this is important. But how much of the time is this really the case? If the situation isn't truly urgent or danger-ous, or if it's happening only in our heads, it might be-hoove us to slow down and take a breath before responding. Even then, the best response may be no response.

Sally Winston, PhD, and Marty Seif, PhD, call this "paradoxical effort." Whether in their books, on pod-casts, or in blogs, they consistently make a distinction between "effort inside the mind" and "effort outside the mind." Moving heavy furniture is the latter. For that, I want to exert maximum effort to lift and move heavy objects. If, however, I'm experiencing butterflies in my stomach and I don't like that, giving attention to that feeling will likely only make things worse.

In the month between getting ghosted and

finding out he had been dating someone else at the same time, I got endless unsolicited advice about checking his Facebook profile, calling him to make sure he wasn't dead, finding an ex-wife, and going to his work. You name it, my friends had to know what was up, and they wanted me to take action. Technically, *they* were being distress intolerant.

I would argue that Alex Honnold, the climber who free-soloed El Capitan, is probably distress tolerant. He is not fearless, but he fears better than ninety-nine percent of us. If you haven't seen the movie "Free Solo", you must. It's incredible. El Cap is 7,573 feet tall, and he climbed it without ropes while being filmed. If he fell, he would have died. In this case, the danger was very real, but he appeared calm. Here's what he's said about fear:

"I feel like fear has this, like an overstated impact on people. And I'm like, why don't people treat fear the same way they treat hunger? Where it's your body showing you, like basically giving you some information. But like when people experience hunger is their body telling 'em that it needs nourishment at some point, but most people just set that aside and then they eat lunch whenever it's convenient. But with fear, most people experience fear, which is basically their body telling 'em that they're, they could be in danger, but then they immediately freak out and act on it. Or, you know, basically it takes over their, what takes over their cognitive process. You know, they're like, "Holy shit, I'm afraid." You know? And I'm like, why can't people set fear aside the same way they set aside hunger and then deal with it when it's appropriate?"

When he references treating fear like hunger, as just "some information," what he's referring to is discerning true danger from false danger. False danger doesn't feel good; it's uncomfortable. But it's not dangerous, and it requires a different response. Noticing the difference so you can shift your reaction is what makes all the difference. Instead of focusing on the discomfort and zooming in (or gripping), we need to learn to widen the perspective and zoom out. That's how you learn to fear better.

When you're in eradication or mitigation mode of your distress, however, the result is the same: temporary relief. Had I done any of those things my friends were suggesting, I might have had a couple minutes (at best) where I felt better, but I probably would have felt even worse afterwards. I'd still feel all the emotions around what happened (that's the pain), plus the guilt of having given in and calling, plus the reminder that he moved on (that's the suffering). And, through it all, I was sane enough to know that a MOFO that duplicitous wasn't going to pick up the phone when I called and suddenly be honest and accountable.

The move we want to start making is letting distress be there, but focusing our attention on something else while it is. We want to practice zooming out as often as possible.

MENTAL FITNESS SKILL #7
Zooming In and Zooming Out

Like bench pressing, this skill is foundational. It operates on the premise that whatever you put your attention on grows and intensifies.

Think of an itch. Sometimes even hearing the word "itch" or "lice" or "bed bugs" can cause me to feel itchy. If you focus on the itch, it gets itchier, and you begin to notice itches in other parts of your body. That's zooming in. When we feel distressed or uncomfortable, our perspective narrows. We get tunnel vision. That's zooming in. What we want to practice in those moments is broadening our perspective to get distance and clarity (that's zooming *out*).

Instead of focusing on the itch, can we focus on other things happening around us? What happens when we do this? When we're distressed or uncomfortable, focusing on whatever we're uncomfortable with will only make it worse. It can be helpful to intentionally step back and notice what else is going on around you. Are there things going well you may be overlooking? Can you place your attention on some of those and make them the louder voice in your head?

To practice, set your timer for five to six minutes and get itchy. If you're like me, this will take two seconds. Instead of scratching the itch, notice it and intentionally place your awareness on something else (zooming out). What else do you see? What else do you hear? What do you feel underneath you? When your brain wants to zoom back into the itch, notice it and zoom back out. Can you be present to what's around you while you experience those sensations? Can you treat the sensations differently?

PRACTICE NOTES

What was this like for you? Did anything surprise you? What happens when you don't make getting rid of the feeling the goal? What opportunities can you find to practice this ASAP and ongoing? How can you hold yourself accountable for practicing this?

Once you get this process down, it's the same idea with thoughts or memories we are scratching too much (zooming in on). When we notice this, we need to stop the behavior, choke up on the leash (in other words, get to the present) and intentionally choose to place our attention somewhere else.

Initially, you'll want to practice this when you're not too upset, so you can feel it out and get the technique down. As always, expect to feel clumsy as you're learning. The more you practice, the easier it will be. Consistency is key.

MENTAL FITNESS SKILL #8
Riding the Wave 2.0 (or Urge Surfing)

I'm assuming you've been practicing riding the wave from Chapter 6 (Mental Fitness Skill #4) and zooming in and zooming out (Mental Fitness Skill #7). If not, build some muscle there before taking on more difficulty. Riding the wave is all about learning to surf our emotions and our urges.

In this exercise, we are going to use the same urge surfing skills but add more distress (though I still want the distress level to be relatively low). Generally, people pick activities like not checking their notifications right when they get them, not responding to messages right away (unless it's truly urgent), choosing what they'd like for dinner instead of asking everyone else what they want first, or not scratching every itch they have for a designated period of time. We're intentionally starting with something extremely low on the distress and discomfort scale in order to learn the technique. Remember, it's all a matter of scale.

Set your timer for twenty or so minutes and commit to getting uncomfortable. When you start to get uncomfortable, notice the urges as they arise. Notice if you start focusing on your discomfort (zooming in). If you do, gently move your awareness to something else (zooming out). What else do you see, what do you hear, what do you smell, what else is going on in your field of awareness? What else is happening in the room? When your brain wants to zoom back in, gently redirect it outward over and over until the urge can peak and pass.

PRACTICE NOTES

What was this like for you? Did anything surprise you? What happens when you don't make getting rid of the feeling the goal? What opportunities can you find to practice this ASAP and ongoing? How can you hold yourself accountable for practicing this?

WINS

CHAPTER 9

"Let It Go."

One of the more common phrases I hear is "I know, I need to let this go." But there's a subtle substitution I always encourage people to make, and that's replacing "go" with "be." When we say, "Let it go," it implies that we need to get rid of something, that we need to *do* something instead of just *allowing* the uncomfortable thoughts, feelings, or sensations to be there *as* we take action.

In this chapter, you're going to put all the pieces together and start doing distress differently. Before we begin, I just want to remind you that what I'm going to suggest going forward has nothing to do with adding tools to your toolkit, exercising, healthy eating or coping skills. This is not going to be about learning a bunch of techniques and hoping you never feel bad again (though I of course hope you don't!). Don't get me wrong, there's nothing inherently wrong with exercise, eating kale, or having tools in your toolkit, but we need to consider WHY we're using those tools.

If you're using them to get rid of a thought or emotion, that's not recommended, for the reasons I've already mentioned. On the other hand, if you're using them to help you stay in the game or because you like any or all of them, go for it.

Take breathing exercises as an example. When I experience intense emotions (as in, daily), I will use interval breathing to keep myself in the present versus hijacked by some crazy possibility my brain has thrown up. I don't use the exercises "to relax," to make the thoughts go away, or to feel better. If any of that happens as a result, great, but that's not the intent. All too often, we think we need to *do* something whenever we're *feeling* something. Remember, the *doing* is the problem; we're getting into the *allowing* game.

What exactly are we allowing? Whatever the stuff is in our heads that we don't like. It could be thoughts, memories, images, emotions, or sensations. We want to do (allow) all of that differently.

If you spend too many hours trying to figure out why someone may not have texted you back, you want to allow the uncertainty as you stop trying to figure it out.

If you dread public speaking, you want to allow the dread as you practice speaking in public.

If you avoid the gym because you're self-conscious of your appearance, you will practice going to the gym as you allow those feelings to be there.

If you typically bring your kids' stuff to them

when they forget it, you'll allow your discomfort as you let your kids experience the natural consequences.

That's what allowing *could* look like, yet you're probably still wondering exactly how one does that differently since you've no doubt already tried 862 approaches. But, if any of them worked consistently, you wouldn't be reading this book! So I'd like to propose something new, and that something I refer to as The ALLOW Principle. It's kind of like Janet Jackson's song "Pleasure Principle," but better, and if the song pops into your head in moments when you need to employ it, I'm okay with that!

Make no mistake, these are principles that you have to feel your way into, so take your time with them and simply commit to a regular practice of them.

Are you gripping (or "lost in your sauce")? Notice when this is happening.

Leash: Choke up on the leash! Return to the present moment using your senses.

Loosen your grip, not the leash (rag doll your body, lengthen your breath, open your hands). Remind your brain: discomfort, not danger.

Out. Zoom out! What else is happening around you, outside of your head?

What matters? Take action toward what matters while you feel however you feel. When you notice you're gripping or back in your head, go back to step two. Repeat.

Here's a visual to help you remember The AL-LOW Principle:

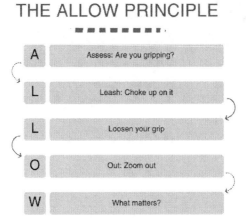

THE ALLOW PRINCIPLE

A	Assess: Are you gripping?
L	Leash: Choke up on it
L	Loosen your grip
O	Out: Zoom out
W	What matters?

In practice, increasing your distress intolerance will probably look a bit more like this:

How to Increase Your Distress Tolerance

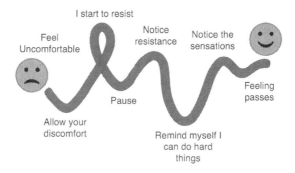

If you're like many of my clients, this may sound both too simple and incredibly confusing at the same time. I find it's easier to understand if practiced with neutral stimuli first.

MENTAL FITNESS SKILL #9

Relaxing into Discomfort (Practicing The ALLOW Principle)

Read the instructions before you get into position or have them next to you so you can read them while you're engaging in the exercise.

Stand up and try to touch your toes (or do it from a seated position). Take a moment to notice what happens when you first start reaching toward your toes.

Observe the sensations in your hamstrings and lower back. Notice what thoughts you attach to those sensations. What happens to your breath when you first start reaching? As you continue reaching further?

Now, I want you to hang out there for another minute or 2.

What do you notice now about your ability to touch your toes? Your breath? What about your thoughts or how you're feeling? Are you able to relax more into the stretch?

How would you describe the transition from the moment before you attempted to touch your toes to the moment when you were fully relaxed, more comfortably touching your toes?

If nothing happened or changed for you, that's okay. Most people, when they first try to touch their toes, aren't able to do so. Their muscles aren't warmed up, so they contract (not knowing if this situation is okay or not). When this happens, their breath gets shorter and shallower, and they may react with negative thoughts about their age, flexibility, or self-discipline for not doing more yoga. When advised to stay there for another minute, relaxing into the pose and focusing on lengthening their breath, their muscles relax and their flexibility increases. *They are relaxing into the discomfort. They are ALLOWing (in the present moment, softening their breath, sending messages of safety to the brain allowing the muscles to relax).*

Another example to consider is getting into a cold

pool. Are you someone who just jumps right in or goes in slowly, gradually getting used to water? Either way, our muscles and breath initially contract, but the more we relax, the faster we adjust. It's not that the temperature increases and that's why it suddenly feels better. We relax and shift our focus away from how cold it is, onto something else, and it feels better.

I know what you're thinking. "Sure, Joanna, anyone can do it with a stretch or a warm-up, but how is that going to help me do the *really* hard thing I want to do?" Or, "I can do it with a stretch, but I can't when…" In either case, my response is the same. Of course you can't…*yet*. And then I'll ask you, "Can you run to the end of your block?" I'm guessing you can. But can you run a half marathon (or 10k or ultra-marathon)? Probably not today, but that doesn't mean you're not inherently capable of doing it.

Here's the seed I want to plant: The process of getting comfortable being uncomfortable—whether the discomfort is physical, mental, or emotional—is the same no matter what, but some experiences/situations will be predictably and significantly more challenging. It's a matter of scale. The same process is just as effective in each instance, it's just employed at different points along the distress continuum. Running a 5k requires the same training process as running a half marathon; one is simply more difficult, mentally and physically.

When discomfort is emotional, not physical, it

may *feel* harder to work through because your thoughts are married with unpleasant and uncomfortable feelings and sensations, but to your body, it's the same, and we can therefore approach it in the same way.

Depending on the situation, your threshold for tolerating discomfort may vary. This is what I refer to as the Sliding Scale of Distress. For our purposes, you want to have a sense where a given situation/experience falls on *your* scale. The higher up the scale you rank a situation/experience, the more predictably challenging it is to manage (think bigger, stronger waves).

Of course it would be much easier if there were a "Couch to 5k" app for allowing distress, but there's not. Essentially that's what you're creating with your scale. Think of the scale as your roadmap. It informs you about where you are and where you're heading. Think of 10 as your ultimate goal (being able to tolerate something that, today, gives you a distress level of 10), 5 as an achievable goal with some effort, and between 0-5 as where you are now.

Anything over 8 *right now* may be outside your "window of tolerance" or point where your flight/fright/freeze/faint system kicks in. You want to avoid starting there since you won't get the learning you need; your survival system will be leading you. As you get more comfortable allowing distress, you'll feel more confident approaching those types of situations.

Willingness: the secret sauce to allowing distress and discomfort. The serenity prayer sums it up pretty well:

"God, grant me the serenity to accept the things I cannot change, the courage to change the things I can, and the wisdom to know the difference."

Willingness or acceptance is *allowing* the present moment, *exactly as it is*. For our purposes, that means not judging whether you like it, whether it's how it "should" be, or whether it's how you want it to be. Just let whatever it is, be.

It's often gray in Cleveland. I've lived here for long enough to know that, yet I still find myself complaining about it every March when we haven't seen the sun in weeks. I get frustrated with the weather and why I'm still here, and I find myself in an awfully unpleasant headspace. In those moments, my willingness is low, but my reality is that the weather is what it is. No amount of hating or complaining changes the weather. Resisting what is just makes me—and those around me—unhappy, because I'm in a foul mood and complain a lot. I'd therefore be better off accepting what is *while* planning a vacation somewhere sunny!

Acceptance is always easier when life is going well. If we're talking about something like the weather, being willing to allow the unpleasant and uncomfortable internal experiences that come with it can feel more difficult because we have no control over it. As much as you may dislike the way you feel or whatever uncomfortable thoughts are in your head, fighting their presence only makes it worse. Instead, practice simply letting them be.

MENTAL FITNESS SKILL #10
Create Your Sliding Scale of Distress

Ally came to see me because she felt like she "could never turn off her brain and just be." She had started going to yoga and loved everything but the two minutes at the end of class where they were instructed to lie silently in savasana (corpse pose). It was a struggle to lie still.

As a busy person, she was constantly multitasking and never felt like she was fully engaged in anything. Every Friday night, her family had a great tradition where they'd order pizza, watch a movie, and make homemade popcorn on the stove. Her son even wrote about how much he loved the tradition for one of his school essays. Ally's experience on Friday nights, however, was quite different. While she loved being with her family, she shamefully bemoaned that "all that stillness is going to kill me." For her, sitting down to eat dinner and watch a movie was that difficult. And no, she did not have ADHD.

The truth, as we came to understand it, was that her busyness was, in part, a way to manage her worry over whether everyone would have a good time, get along, and uphold the happy tradition (outcome focus). Part of her busyness was not liking how the worry felt, so she would distract herself by always doing (and there's no shortage of stuff for moms to do). It was hard to follow conversations, let alone a movie plot, because she was always thinking of the next thing she had to do. Her watch then inevitably vibrated, at which point she *had* to check who had emailed. She then began problem-solving something that could absolutely wait until Monday, but why not think about it now? This pattern continued to repeat itself, and her life was running on a tank of anxious busyness.

When I asked her how she'd know if therapy was effective, her answer was, "I'd be able to have a 'digital sabbath' from Friday after work until Saturday morning." It wasn't *just* that she wanted a break from electronics. She also wanted to be fully present with her family instead of being with them physically but not being engaged because she was so in her head. Without her phone to distract her, she was going to have to learn how to feel a lot of feelings: uncertainty, boredom, worry, guilt, irresponsibility, and agitation, to name a few. She was going to have to learn that she could experience these feelings and sensations *and* that it didn't mean that anything was wrong or urgent, or that the feelings would last forever. That just because the situation felt important didn't mean it *was* important, would last forever, or would ruin the night.

Toward that end, here was her scale:

10: No electronics Friday night (digital sabbath)

8: No electronics from 5pm to bedtime

7.5: Run errands without phone or watch

5: Do not disturb during work hours

3: No electronics during meals

1: No electronics before work

The goal wasn't to feel calm on Friday night without her phone. The goal was to feel however she felt while she was present with her family. It wasn't either/or anymore. She learned she could feel any feeling, have any thought or sensation, *and* still be present. Also, she learned that her family members had a lot more fun when she wasn't on her phone and could sit with them instead of scurrying around.

Now for the million-dollar question: How do you put this all together and get started?

It's time to create your own Sliding Scale of Distress for a specific situation or experience you're presently struggling with. Identify the discomfort you can commit to leaning into, over and over again. Start with situations/experiences that are low enough on the scale (4-5 range) that you can do them pretty easily, *and* make sure they are situations/experiences you can practice repeatedly. Don't pick situations that happen infrequently or unpredictably, because you won't get the practice needed to strengthen your distress tolerance muscle.

In general, your scale will contain

experiences/situations that fit the following parameters related to a specific goal:

9-10: These are the situations/experiences that, right now, you can't imagine tolerating at all. They're just too hard. If you engaged in these, your body would likely flood with adrenaline, and you'd be immediately outside your window of tolerance.

7-8: These are the situations/experiences that are still quite hard to do without lots of resistance to feelings, but they're not completely outside your window of tolerance.

5-6: These are the situations/experiences that you could do while practicing allowance of the feelings that come with them. They'd be tough, but they're doable.

3-4: These are the situations/experiences that are low-distress situations and therefore great starting points for practicing an allowing mindset.

If your goal is to get to the gym four days a week after work, but you feel dread every time you think about going (so you bail), what you need to build is dread tolerance. Here's what your scale might look like in that case:

10: Working out at a peak distress time (after work in this case)

9: Having a training session (where you're accountable to a trainer) during a peak time

8: Working out before work when it's a bit less crowded

7: Working out with a friend when the gym opens

6: Attending a scheduled session with a trainer when the gym opens

5: Taking a class during the day

4: Working out for a very short period of time

3: Taking a tour of the gym

The specific numbers don't really matter, so don't overthink that part. You're going for a rough range. The practice is to do distress/dread differently (remember process-focus versus outcome-focus). Instead of trying to control the outcome, the practice is to allow the dread to be there without making it the loudest voice in your head. Can you feel dread as you go to the gym and keep driving without turning back toward your house? Can you feel the dread *and* do the things that move you toward what matters?

Margaret came to see me because she was feeling "burned out" in all areas of her life. She felt like she had overextended herself professionally because she was scared she would be passed over if she didn't please her bosses. She overextended herself at her kids' school because she didn't want to seem like an uninvolved parent. She let her friends dictate plans and restaurant choices to minimize disagreements, and she struggled to set appropriate parental boundaries with her kids because she didn't want them throwing fits when the family was finally all together.

After unpacking her history and current situation, one of the patterns she identified was putting other people's needs first to avoid potential conflict and internal discomfort. She wanted to stop her people-pleasing patterns and start saying no more often. Here are some of the situations/experiences that went on her scale:

10: Being consistent with bedtime routines so the kids were in bed by 8pm

9: Saying no to chaperoning the upcoming field trip

8.5: Not rereading emails five times before she sent them at work

7.5: Not saying "I'm sorry" compulsively (when she bumped into people at the grocery store, asked her assistant to do something, or couldn't do something at her kids' school)

7: Not intentionally leaving work after her bosses had already left

6.5: Suggesting an alternate plan with her friends instead of just going with theirs

5: Not asking her family what they want for dinner, just choosing it

4: Not allowing her kids to have electronics in the car or at meals

3: Buying a treat for her kids' school party instead of making one

Like anyone who takes on behavior change, her trajectory was several steps forward, then a few steps back. Evaluating her progress based on how she felt she was doing more of what mattered was a radical change for her. Without realizing it, she was extremely used to reacting to how she was feeling and thinking. With our plan in place, she began paying more attention to what she wanted to do, what was important to her, and what actions moved her toward what mattered.

Since she was no longer feeling overextended and exhausted, she had more space for family and friends. And, by learning to comfortably set boundaries at home, she was also able to begin setting them at work and accepting whatever uncertainty came with doing so. Learning to do discomfort differently was worth it for the life that opened up to her as a result.

Margaret contacted me a couple years after we stopped working together, thanking me for "shifting her attitude about discomfort." Learning to *allow* the discomfort helped her move from an attitude of resisting to expanding.

Sometimes the behaviors are things we do outside our heads. Sometimes they're things we do *inside* our heads. Sometimes, it's a mix of the two. Case in point, about six weeks after I was ghosted, I found out this guy had a girlfriend during the entirety of our "relationship." A friend of mine sent me a screenshot when they went Facebook official. Of course I wanted to text him, text her, comment on their pictures, and defame him publicly, but I didn't do anything of the sort. For the most part, I tried not to ask my friends for reassurance around any number of questions I had (behavior outside my head), since I knew they didn't have the answers I was seeking.

What was happening *inside* my head, however, was a different story. I was exhausting myself with pointless mental gymnastics, trying to answer unanswerable questions. I was making myself sick, spinning and churning, trying so hard to make sense of what had happened. In order to stop torturing myself, I had to stop all those sneaky mental behaviors. Here was a smattering of my scale:

10: Any interaction with him

9: Listen to Kendrick Lamar without replaying memories or trying to answer questions

8.5: Date someone without excessively worrying whether he was going to ghost me

7.5: Resist the urge to date someone who admitted to having ever ghosted someone

7: Resist the urge to check his Facebook profile and ruminate about what happened

6: Try to figure out (for the hundredth time) how he could be so duplicitous

5: Resist the urge to beat myself up for missing the red flags

4: Resist the urge to replay every date to identify

every red flag I missed

Regardless of which situation I was managing, the source of my pain always came down to two things: uncertainty tolerance and the need to make space for a lot of sad feelings. I came to understand that it wasn't *him* I missed, it was hope I missed. It didn't mean I couldn't feel hope ever again, but I had to acknowledge what was present at that time. Now when a memory pops up, it still stings, but less, and I know the source of it, so I can ride it more easily.

MENTAL FITNESS SKILL #11
Get (More) Comfortable With Discomfort

Rationale for the skill: Now is the time to start putting it all together (and practicing The ALLOW Principle). LFG (Let's Fucking Go—for my mom, who will have no idea what that stands for). Now that you have your scale, some skills at your disposal, and a felt sense of how to relax into discomfort, it's "go" time.

Pick a situation/experience between 4 and 5 on your scale that's something you can practice regularly. If the 4s seem too much, pick a 3.5 action. Before you do it, I want you to get in the right headspace. For anything that's important, prepare as much as is feasible versus winging it. Consider the following questions:

- Am I clear about what I'm trying to do?

- How can I remember to practice The ALLOW Principles when I feel uncomfortable? (For example, do I need to write them out or have a note in my phone I can reference?)
- When things get hard, what I want to remember is [insert your "why" from chapter 4]. (This may not be applicable now, but it will be at some point.)

Once you've done that, it's time to take the plunge. Remember, progress is not based on the presence or absence of thoughts or feelings, since those are out of your control. Progress is based on how you *respond* to those thoughts and feelings. Can you continue to let them be, zoom out, and focus on other things? Are you spending less time in your head and more time in life?

PRACTICE NOTES

How did it go? Did anything surprise you? How can you commit to practicing this consistently? Since we cannot unlearn stuff, the only way to create new learning is by incorporating a lot of repetition. Doing this once isn't going to cut it. We need as many opportunities in as many situations as possible for the brain to learn that you can feel all levels of distress and discomfort, and it doesn't mean anything is wrong. It may suck, but you're okay. It may be hard, and you can still do it.

WINS

PART 2

Everything That Could Go Wrong
(AND HOW TO COURSE CORRECT)

N ow the *real* fun begins. I've laid out a process to help you lean into distress and discomfort, and now it's all about practicing. I know that's not a very sexy next step, but it's the best possible one.

You need a lot of practice to get a feel for this stuff and make some deposits into your experience and confidence banks. And, like any new skill, it's not going to feel natural, intuitive, or easy right away. You'll still be in your head, trying to remember what to do most of the time. It's like dancing—the more you "try to dance" by thinking about each step and where to put your arms and legs, the more you'll suck. With dancing, you need a basic sense of what to do, and then you need to let your body just move. This is no different.

I've given you the basic steps when it comes to strengthening your distress tolerance muscles. Now it's time to get out of your head and move. Remember, we're playing the long game, and meaningful change takes time, patience, and self-compassion.

Here's where you're in luck. Not only have I been a therapist for a long time, but I've gotten in my own way for even longer. So I am well-versed in things that can get in your way. While I can't think of *everything* that may go wrong and every way you may get in your own way, I've thought of many and how you can course correct from each.

CHAPTER 10

MISHAP #1
Thinking You're a Failure When You "Fail"

The Lululemon execs got it right when they put "Life is full of setbacks. Success is determined by how you handle setbacks" on one of their bags. When I speak of failure, I'm referring to setbacks, mistakes, or any time you think you fucked up. Over the years, I've had different relationships with failure. I spent most of my life married to the idea that if I failed at something, it meant that *I* was a failure. Because of my perception early on in life that I sucked at almost everything I did, I felt horribly about myself for a long time. Once I learned how to separate my self-worth from the experience of "failure" and see it as an opportunity for growth, the word lost its sting.

Confusing an unpleasant experience (a disagreement in a relationship, challenge at a job, or unpleasant conversation with a friend) with being a failure is a great example of conflating an outcome with a judgment of the outcome. Remember Mental Fitness Skill #1: Just the facts, ma'am? The objective fact in that instance was that my husband and I were divorcing. My interpretation of the situation was that I failed as a wife, and I failed at marriage. The divorce was painful, yes, but all the shit I layered onto it made it worse.

When we have this attitude about failure, we tend to look at situations in black-and-white terms. I was either married and good, or divorced and a failure. That kind of thinking is also called all-or-nothing or either/or thinking, and the point is that it's binary. You've either won or lost, made it or not. Not only does this attitude negate the gray but it also focuses exclusively on the outcome, which, many times, you cannot control. So many other things (how we communicated, how we navigated conflict, how we loved, and our respective processes) get lost.

Once I got enough distance, had enough therapy (yes, therapists sometimes need therapy too!), and consumed enough Esther Perel, PhD, I was able to notice when that story came up (I called it my "shitty wife story") and leave it be. Then I could gain a new perspective and see the enormous part the other person played, what did go well, and how many wins I collected along the way. Eventually, I was able to see that we did work well together as parents, and I wasn't as terrible as I thought. All of that learning and awareness prepared me for other relationships and for being willing to be vulnerable again (even if it did bring about a hard right with the ghosting incident, but there were lessons to be learned there as well.) Seeing failure as an opportunity is an essential part of a growth mindset.

Side note: I can't believe Lululemon *hasn't* put "Embrace failure" on a bag or coffee mug. Given my disdain for word art, I would never buy it, but I'm all for the message.

Instead of viewing setbacks (or "failures") as permanent roadblocks or character flaws, imagine looking at them as opportunities to get stronger. By changing your perspective on missteps and setbacks, you can actually learn from those experiences while also staying true to who you are, no matter what life throws at you. That's what failing forward is all about. Learn to view setbacks as simply part of the growth process.

Sometimes, it's easier to gain experience with this where you least expect it. For me, it was when I started powerlifting. My first big lifting goal was to bench "plates," or 135 pounds. I set the goal when I started seriously lifting in March 2020. At the time, I could only bench eighty pounds, and I had no idea it would take me nineteen months to reach this goal. There were months I was on fire, feeling great, and then, for months, I couldn't get past 110 pounds. For six months straight, the goal to lift 135 pounds felt *just* out of my reach. Not only were my muscles failing, but too often I felt like a failure. I couldn't believe how long I could be stuck on the same weight. There had to be something wrong with me.

Once I developed the strength to bench 110 pounds consistently, the next small goal appeared. At this level, the weight always felt heavy. My trainer said this would happen—that I'd get to a certain strength level where every lift was objectively hard and uncomfortable. At this point, I was benching weights at a volume I couldn't always even finish. I became accustomed to bad days, bad weeks, and even bad months.

Over the course of nineteen months, I hit enough lows to learn that there was no limit to the number of bad days you could have at the gym. Eighty-five percent of the problem was mental. I was getting in my head, telling myself I couldn't do it before I even tried, and giving in to the fear when I started to struggle. If the slightest thing felt off—something didn't feel just right or my breath was off or my timing was off—I couldn't do it.

I had to find a way to ignore those voices and make another voice louder (zooming in versus zooming out). That's how I got out of my head and broke the slump. That was the foothold I needed. From there, it's been a process of practice, tweak, repeat. Moving my feet, making sure my shoulders are situated properly, ensuring I'm pushing into the bench enough and bracing enough, and double-checking my grip and what my elbows are doing.

The way I approach lifting's setbacks is the same way I approach life's setbacks. Even the most challenging setbacks can offer valuable lessons about ourselves and our capabilities, and we can use these experiences to recognize what went wrong and then make adjustments.

These are the four "rules" I've found to be most helpful:

1. Be gentle with yourself.
2. Find the lesson.
3. Tweak your process (if there's something you can adjust).
4. Stay consistent. There will be other chances to practice and succeed.

WINS

CHAPTER 11

MISHAP #2
Judging Yourself

One could argue that this chapter should be at the start of the book since it's so important. I'll be honest, when I first heard about the idea of self-compassion, I immediately thought of the Stuart Smalley skits from SNL. I could not imagine myself standing in front of a mirror saying, "I'm good enough, I'm smart enough, and doggone it, people like me." I still can't. And yet, I'm a firm believer that this is a muscle we need to strengthen.

I used to think self-compassion was intuitive and, therefore, one more thing I lacked. Like a maternal instinct or fashion sense. It became one more thing I could beat myself up for not having or for sucking at. But here's the thing: self-compassion is absolutely a skill you can both learn and get better at with practice. As Brené Brown explains, "Compassion is not a virtue—it is a commitment. It's not something we have or don't have—it's something we choose to practice."

I want to be very clear about the fact that I am nowhere close to being an expert in self-compassion. I am an expert in self-criticism. I could blame it on my heavy Virgo placements, perfectionist parents from the East Coast, or history of anxiety disorders, but realistically it's because I've had a habit of beating myself up for as long as I can remember, and it caused me a lot of suffering.

Having self-compassion is critical these days because most of us speak so horribly to ourselves. If we think of self-criticism and self-compassion as muscles, most of us have overdeveloped self-criticism muscles and underdeveloped self-compassion muscles. It's like those guys at the gym with huge chests and small legs. When we consider that language shapes our reality, it takes this concept to a whole new level.

Self-compassion is one of the hardest skills I've had to learn. Pull-ups with weights tied to my ankles may be easier. Not only did I not know what words to string together to be nice to myself, I didn't know how it would feel to receive that, and I was scared to enjoy it because it might not last. Disappointment might be around the corner. Sometimes, choosing to be kind to myself feels harder than beating myself up. Self-criticism is familiar; I know what to expect. Yes, it feels shitty, but it's a known entity. There are no surprises.

In the beginning, self-compassion felt so foreign

that I thought I was going to crawl out of my skin. While there are still some situations where I'm still "sticky" when it comes to beating myself up and I have to work really hard to pull myself out of the rabbit hole, I've grown to the point where, more times than not (and in most situations), I can show myself a lot of grace.

Andrea is a typical client of mine. She works full-time in a demanding job, has young kids, manages to get to yoga a couple times a week, and somehow cooks a homemade dinner every night. I couldn't do one-tenth of what she does in a week, but to her, she's not doing any of it well enough. To her, she should be doing more, producing more, being more present, and being more involved. Her inner critic has always been a constant voice in her head, making her profoundly miserable.

When I suggested there were ways to quiet the critic, she looked at me, dumbfounded and confused. She thought it would be "letting herself off the hook" to be easier on herself. That being gentler with herself was somehow "giving her a pass to not care." She couldn't imagine a middle ground where she could "keep her edge" but not berate herself with criticisms during most of her waking moments. Thankfully, she was willing to humor me and give it a try.

When I asked her to say just one kind thing to herself, she couldn't come up with anything. She was completely speechless. She remarked that the kind words she'd say to a friend didn't sound like anything she could possibly say to herself (there was a different set of rules for her friends than for herself), so she landed on "You're doing what you can right now and that's okay." (We settled on "what you can" instead of "the best you can" because, as she saw it, she wasn't doing the best she could. That was the problem!)

It wasn't until Andrea learned about the data supporting a self-compassion practice that she was really willing to do it. There is a lot of scientific evidence to support the benefits of being nicer to oneself. Research indicates that self-compassion is strongly associated with psychological well-being. Additionally, according to the National Institute of Health, higher levels of self-compassion are linked to increased feelings of happiness, optimism, curiosity, and connectedness, as well as decreased anxiety, depression, rumination, and fear of failure.

When you're not spending time and energy berating yourself for your mistakes, you can acknowledge them, tweak your process, and move on. People who are more self-compassionate don't view mistakes as moral failings; they view them as universal experiences and opportunities to grow.

There is no one right way to practice being kinder to yourself. What's important is that you do it, and do it often. Besides being demoralizing and generally unmotivating (as if those aren't reasons enough), when you're hating on yourself, you're also closed off to anything that might be working or going well. And the longer you've been greasing those wheels, the easier it is for your brain to slip into those grooves. If you want to show your brain something different (for example, that you don't completely suck), you have to be intentional about it.

Injecting grace and self-kindness is helpful whenever we're doing something new or difficult, but it's also a good muscle to work in general.

Here are some resources and action steps to get you started:

- Read or otherwise engage with anything by Kristin Neff, PhD, Chris Germer, PhD, or Sharon Salzberg. They are all leaders in the field of self-compassion and/or loving kindness meditation (I'm sure there are others, but these are the experts I've turned to most).

- Notice when you're beating yourself up. Ask yourself, "How can I show myself some grace in this instance?" Ask yourself, "What would I say to my kids or a dear friend?" if you're having trouble figuring out how to offer yourself kindness.

- Remind yourself that the feeling is temporary.

When I was learning, my therapist advised me to say to myself, "Joanna, stop. I am not going down this road again. There is nothing helpful or useful in saying this to myself."

WINS

CHAPTER 12

MISHAP #3

Settling For "Good Enough" Change

(TACKLING ONLY PART OF YOUR SCALE)

I know almost nothing about sports except the juicy gossip I read online. The only piece of baseball knowledge I have came from dating someone who had season tickets to the Guardians, so I went to a lot of games. Honestly, it was too much, but I did learn that the best batter typically bats third. In that spirit, I'm putting the concept of settling for the "good enough" change third because it's that important to consider.

As a therapist on the front lines of treating people's health and contamination concerns during Covid, I had a front-row seat to how the pandemic upended people's lives, routines, and mental health. As I write this in early 2023, many people have gone back to living their "normal" life, however it may have been reshaped. But there are still so many who are struggling to reintegrate back into life. I see this every day as a therapist specializing in treating OCD and anxiety disorders. For many, treatment has been a negotiation of how much they want to push themselves, how much "risk" they want to take, and how much they think they can handle. It's important to note that *none* of the people about whom I'm referring are in a high-risk group and/or living with anyone in a high-risk group.

Today, their life is filled with statements such as:

- I'll vacation, but only if it's within driving distance.
- I'll go out to eat, but only if it's outside or the place isn't crowded (they live in Cleveland, not Florida).
- I'll go to stores if there's no chance of long lines.
- I'll only go into the office if I am masked, wiping down surfaces, and having hand sanitizer at meetings.
- I'm not going out. (They've given up many activities because it feels like "too much." This includes going to the movie theater (even matinees), traveling, and going to the gym (with the excuse that they're saving money by doing it at home, even though they loved the social part).

In the therapy office, I call this a "conditioned or contingent recovery." Your recovery is contingent on having certain things in place. I can do X *if* Y is present.

For our purposes, we can also call it the "good enough change." This person changed enough that they can function. Their life is a lot better than when they started, but they will only take it so far. They still believe there's stuff they can't handle, emotions that are "too much," and situations that are "too dangerous."

The exceptions they've put into place are ones they can live with. Anyone can maneuver his or her life to the point where they never have to fly, go to a concert, or go on a cruise. But what happens if you have to fly for work? Or you have to wait in line, and you don't have your Xanax (or your mints, phone, or other "coping tools")? Or your plans change, and you don't have time to do whatever you normally do to feel okay. Or your kids want to do fun stuff? Or your partner wants to go out? It's one thing to pretzel yourself, but how does it impact those around you?

I completely understand the urge to forgo your hardest stuff, and it's from personal experience that I'm telling you, don't do it! Think of every opportunity you practice as a deposit you make into your confidence bank. You'll want to have made as many deposits as possible when life throws you curveballs, which will inevitably happen.

Again, don't start practicing with the experiences and situations that sit at 8-10 on your tolerance scale, but once you're ready, make sure you do them. You never want to say, "I can get through anything but…" or "So long as this doesn't happen, I'm good." Here are some of the 8- to 10-level activities on my own scale I've worked on over the years:

- Doing sprint time trials at the end of a grueling Crossfit workout (I always considered it too intimidating)
- Seeing my ex-husband with his new wife (then girlfriend)
- Flying without "just in case" Xanax
- Going back into a mall after being involved in an attempted shooting
- Opening myself up to love again

TIPS FOR TACKLING TOP-OF-THE-SCALE EXPERIENCES/SITUATIONS

Work up to these situations/experiences! If you do any of them soon, you'll likely get flooded with adrenaline and lose the learning. Use the same process you used for lower-level activities on the tolerance scale. 8- to 10-level experiences are no different from 3- to 5-level experiences, beyond the fact that they are predictably more challenging. Think of it as lifting a heavier weight.

Like anything challenging, practice makes it easier. Don't expect it to feel good, especially not right away; that's unrealistic. Focus on your why. Make sure you give yourself lots of grace as you do it. This is hard stuff!

WINS

CHAPTER 13

MISHAP #4
White-Knuckling

The term "white-knuckling" is perfect for describing doing something while resisting every minute of it. The first time I heard the term, I was about seven, and we were going on a trip. My dad used it to describe the way I was gripping the arm rests as the plane took off. All of my memories of flying involve me being in some state of panic, vomiting (I'm not sure if I was panicked because I was terrified to throw up or throwing up because I was terrified, but the two issues didn't do each other any favors), or asleep after my mom started slipping me Valium "because I had allergies."

Any time I was on the plane (and awake), I was 100 percent terrified of both the experience and my fear. When we're white-knuckling through an experience, we're actually resisting it, thinking "I'm here but hating this." That attitude blocks the learning we want, that "this may suck, *and* I can do it."

This brings us back to the idea of willingness or allowance. I've often said willingness is the "secret sauce" of recovery because if you can accept and allow how you're feeling in any given moment, your symptoms will no longer matter.

So often, when clients tell me they're trying "but it's just not getting any easier," it's often because they're unknowingly white-knuckling.

Other ways white-knuckling shows up:

- Doing the "scary" thing, but telling yourself how much you hate it.
- Doing it with a bad attitude.
- Doing the thing/going to the place, but holding back in some way.
- Being there but remaining closed off (body language is closed, tense).
- Being there but planning your escape plan.
- Doing it but staring at the clock or counting down the minutes until you can leave.
- Being there, but being somewhere else in your head.

Remember, willingness is a process of opening up to your present internal experience exactly as it is. It's about accepting whatever thoughts, urges, memories, feelings, or sensations are showing up in your head in any given moment, exactly as they are. Here's the thing:

- You don't have to like what's there.
- You don't have to agree with it.
- You *do* have to accept that it is taking up space right now in your head.

To try and change what's there is resisting, and that makes it worse. We want to accept the reality that that stuff is there. As I say to my clients, "Accept the campfire. Don't make it a forest fire." It's simple, but not easy. If the discomfort is mild, it's not as hard to do. I can work with a simmering worry, no problem. But if the distress is intense and the fear feels so real and so important (even if it's the same fear that's come up fifty other times this week), it can be harder to allow it.

When you set out to do your stuff, you may find yourself in situations where the discomfort may be higher than you anticipated or you're trying hard to do the task, but it's not getting any easier. Ask yourself if you may be white-knuckling. Is there some part of the experience that you're fighting? Where you might be tensing up or your attitude changes? That may be your tipping point right now.

The next time you do this activity (ideally, the next day), can you try to lean in and see if you can loosen your grip a bit? Is your willingness to allow more intense feelings and sensations growing?

If you notice you're white-knuckling, check your willingness.

Chances are, it's low, so you want to raise it. Remember, you'd rather have a campfire than a forest fire. To increase your willingness, I find it helpful to think of it on a continuum, from 1-10.

10: You're chasing that feeling, wanting more of it. That's how little you care if you feel it.

8: You're allowing the feeling to pass over you. You're not fighting it at all.

6-7: You're ping-ponging between moments of loosening your grip and tightening it back up, glimpsing what it feels like to be in both spaces.

5: You're doing the behavior but white-knuckling in some way.

3-4: You're thinking about doing the behavior, but still engaging in lots of control strategies.

1-3: Your willingness to feel distress or discomfort is low. You're trying really hard to get rid of it.

The key is to notice where you are and then work to loosen your grip, one step at a time. Once we stop fighting, it gets easier, we build momentum, and the small wins become bigger wins.

WINS

CHAPTER 14

MISHAP #5
The Fuck-Its

I see the Fuck-Its occur most often around the new year, when people fall prey to all the aforementioned "New Year, New You" pressure and set really intense goals with no planning or preparation. They jump right into action, giving up alcohol, sugar, carbs, their couch, Netflix, porn—everything they've deemed "bad"—without much, if any, thought about why they might be using it to begin with, how they'll ride out urges, or what will happen when they start to feel feelings they haven't felt in a minute.

Things generally go well for a couple weeks, and then reality hits. Maybe that means they slip off course, feel emotional, or something sets them off, and they think, "Well, the day is blown already so I may as well go for it" or "I can't take this, I'm done" or "It's too much, I'm giving in." However you phrase it, it generally ends with "Fuck it," followed by old behavior.

No, The Fuck-Its isn't a clinical term, but it sure does well-describe the feeling you get when you're trying to make a change and have started to implement a new behavior, but something trips you up (generally some form of distress or discomfort) and sets you off. It could be something you weren't anticipating or simply the difference between your reality and your expectations, but it's enough to make you want to throw in the proverbial towel. That's the moment when you decide to give up the diet and eat a bunch of shit, delete all your apps and stop dating, take off your gym clothes and watch Netflix, or put off starting your new project and take a nap.

When this happens, I'll go out on a limb and guess that the situation itself isn't what triggers your reaction. It's more likely that your behavior (your reaction) is an attempt to regulate a lot of internal discomfort. Whether it's from feeling disappointment, frustration, burnout, anxiousness, worry, or some other emotion that's bubbling up, I'm guessing *that's* the real issue. And, in an attempt to get rid of it, you're likely following a familiar pattern of avoiding.

HOW TO COURSE CORRECT FROM THE FUCK-ITS

Get back on track ASAP! Instead of using the slip-up as permission to go back to old behavior, try getting back on track as soon as you can. That's often the small change that happens as we start to improve: when we get off the path, we can get back on faster.

Check your scale. Sometimes it's a scaling issue (Mental Fitness Skill #10). Perhaps you went too high too fast, or thought something was lower on the scale than it actually was. This is another reason why scaling your desired change is so helpful. Both jumping into action too quickly and starting too high on the scale happen all the time and can sabotage behavior change. I'd rather you start slower and lower, and accumulate wins and confidence so you'll feel more prepared when the harder stuff comes. I know the hard stuff is sexy, but doing it well is even sexier.

Show yourself grace, especially if you're beating yourself up. Change is hard, and it's never linear. Find the learning, be gentle with yourself, and take another step toward your desired change as soon as you can.

Perhaps you're thinking, "Isn't this just a matter of having good habits and discipline?" Both are important and active ingredients of what makes someone successful, but they aren't the only things. I'm much more interested in another active ingredient, one that's often overlooked, which is the strength of someone's distress tolerance muscle (which is precisely what's being called up when maintaining a new habit gets hard and you're faced with uncomfortable feelings). When that happens, when you're at your tipping point, I want you to have a way to *allow* those feelings so you can keep going. (If necessary, refer back to Mental

Fitness Skills #9 and #11.)

WINS

CHAPTER 15

MISHAP #6
The Urgent Need for Self-Care
(AND OTHER DISTRACTIONS)

When I first sat down to write this book, I was told to set a timer for thirty minutes each day and "just write." I would stare at my outline and my blank computer screen and my mind would go blank. My head would throb and my hands would sweat as I searched for the perfect way to say something. The more frustrated I felt, the more distracted I became.

I was distracted by my nails that needed to be cut and filed, eyebrows that needed to be tweezed, wrinkles that needed to be assessed, and split ends that needed to be picked…now. Some days, I needed the right essential oils to boost creativity, so I wasted time googling what those were. Other days, I needed to create the perfect space, so I had to get the right candles and plants. Before I knew it, my thirty-minute alarm went off, announcing that my writing time was over, and I had exactly nothing to show for it. On many of those days, the excuse I used for not sitting down to write was that I was engaging in "self-care." But my "self-care" was really just procrastinating. I was also forgetting that, sometimes, self-care is doing hard things.

There were days along the way when I did need to back off and take a break. I thought of them as my recovery days. The key is to know when to push it and when to back off. Also, when backing off is really procrastination. Here are some questions to consider in order to determine whether you need a recovery day or are procrastinating:

- When is the urge happening (is right as you sit down to write, or more generally)?
- Do you already have rest days planned?
- What's the function of the behavior (are you bailing because you want to avoid a specific feeling)?
- Could this be a good opportunity to lean into the discomfort and do it anyway?

My advice:

- Plan your rest days in advance.
- If it's not a rest day, commit to the activity regardless of how you feel.

- Continue to engage with your new process when the distress hits in order to ride it out.
- Acknowledge the win when you do what you set out to do.

WINS

CHAPTER 16

MISHAP #7
Watering the Weeds
(A.K.A. OVERTHINKING)

Traveling in 2021-2022 was fraught, but not because of cancellations the way it is today. The main issue then was the fear of Covid variants (and contracting one) was still very much on people's minds. If you were brave enough to leave the country, you had to prove your negative status to reenter the US as well as to enter several other countries.

You likely can think of someone who was stranded someplace because they contracted Covid on their vacation. More than the number of people who were actually stranded, however, are the countless numbers I've listened to who spent endless hours worrying about getting stranded, planning for situations that never happened, researching alternate flight options they never needed, avoiding cool excursions because of the potential to be exposed, and generally making themselves and everyone around them miserable because they were so worried about something that *could* happen but didn't.

A common metaphor when thinking about our brains and anxiety is plants in a garden. Whatever you water, grows. Whatever you don't, dies. Any thoughts you're watering with attention are thoughts that are going to grow. This is another reason why practicing self-compassion is important. A lot of people are spending a lot of time watering things that have either already happened, may never happen, or they have no control over one way or the other. **In all cases, the thinking is the behavior we want to target.**

Clients often tell me they didn't realize that thinking or worrying is a behavior, not to mention one in their control. They'll often describe it as "something that just happens" or "something that's out of my control." It may feel that way, but while the thoughts that pop into our heads are not within our control, thinking is a choice. This is important to remember, because anytime we step outside our comfort zone, we may quickly question what we're doing and why we're subjecting ourselves to this. It can be really easy in those moments to start second-guessing ourselves and want to avoid it. We may also start seeking reassurance from friends or want to vent to our partners to make sure we don't seem "off track."

Sometimes we forget that thinking, worrying, ruminating, replaying, fretting, processing, and venting can all be subtle (or not so subtle) ways of resisting reality that, in the end, only make the behavior stronger.

All we're doing is watering the weeds.

Paul was in his mid-twenties when he called me seeking treatment for his social anxiety. He was new to the area and starting his medical residency. As far back as he could remember, he had worried about making a fool of himself or "doing something stupid."

During college, having a heavy course load was the perfect excuse to avoid social opportunities. The few times he reported going to a party or bar, he remembered feeling "too stressed out and in my head to even enjoy it." Since medical school was even more demanding, he could continue to avoid it, though he realized that his peers were having much more fun forming friendships, relationships, and a sense of community of which he was (again) not a part.

When he started his residency, he was determined to do things differently. One of the perks of the residency was a free membership at a beautiful gym. Historically, the gym had been a place he avoided because he was convinced he'd be judged for being too skinny, too weak, and too out of shape. When he first started going, he was in his head the whole time (*Are they looking at me weirdly? Why did they give me that look?*). To offset his fears, he would apologize to the trainers when asking a question about how to use a machine. He would replay conversations in his head to reassure himself he didn't say anything stupid, and he would ask his roommate for reassurance that he didn't do something embarrassing.

What we worked on was cutting out all of those behaviors—the overthinking, the replaying of situations/conversations, seeking reassurance, and giving himself reassurance. In short, he worked on approaching his worry differently. Instead of giving it so much attention, he worked on giving his workout the attention and allowing his thoughts and feelings to just be. He started paying more attention to his music, his breath, and his technique, and less to the worries. It was not easy, *and* it paid off. He started to see that he enjoyed the gym much more when he wasn't focused on what other people may or may not be thinking. He also started meeting people and building a life outside of work.

If you notice you're getting caught in your head:

- Make something else the louder voice (zoom out). Your brain will want to lure you back in with more "what if" thoughts, and your job is to just keep going.
- Bring your awareness back to whatever it is you're doing.
- Ask yourself, "What am I teaching my brain in this moment?" If you're worrying, you're teaching your brain to worry more. If you're showing it that now is the time for reading, it learns to focus on reading.

When you stop responding to your worry

thoughts, your brain will get the message that there's no danger. It will learn that this situation/stimulus is safe. It may take months of practice and repetition, but you *can* retrain your brain (and it may even be easier than teaching your dog or your loved ones new tricks). Hang in there.

WINS

CHAPTER 17

MISHAP #8
Talking Yourself Out of Starting

Online dating. Even writing those two words fills me with dread. (This can't be a surprising revelation at this point.) Perhaps it's the endless car (or bathroom) selfies; or the profiles that extoll Cleveland sports and college football as bellwethers for emotional compatibility; or the chats around weekends, weather, and the combination of the two. Despite all of this, my desire to date often outweighs my dread, so I put myself back online. Every time I've done that, I've talked myself out of it at least three times. My anticipation of the experience is always to blame.

I even had a relationship coach tell me this was a "me problem" (not a revelation) and that I needed to be "psychotically optimistic." The only things I'm even remotely close to psychotically optimistic about are new seasons of "Succession" and the mini-sheepadoodles I follow on Instagram. That being said, learning how to online date differently would probably be quite helpful.

Anytime we have feelings about something before it happens, it's called anticipatory (insert feeling). I hear this most often in relation to anxiety. When you're worrying about something weeks or months before it even happens, that's called anticipatory anxiety. It's important to note that you can also have anticipatory dread, disgust, excitement, or any other emotion. The anticipation of something perceived as "negative" can be so intense that we talk ourselves out of it. The more challenging the situation you're walking into, the more likely it is that it'll happen. But it doesn't have to be a challenging situation for this to occur. It can also be an activity that you simply don't want to do because it's challenging in some kind of way for you. When you're there, what story are you telling yourself about that situation or what could happen? Chances are, your brain has way too much leash!

You may already know this is an issue for you, or it may be one that comes up as you start making some changes. We may think that all the pre-worrying we do is helpful, but it's really not. Plus, the nature of anxiety is always to double down on how bad something will be while underestimating your ability to do it. If anxiety were a friend, it wouldn't be someone you'd want to pregame with, would it?

When we get caught in an anticipatory spiral, we often assume that just because something could happen, it will. When we are anxious or worried, we become experts in "what if" thinking, thinking that's entirely based on a possibility that may not ever happen. You may even start trying to solve problems that will never come to pass. I've talked myself into realities that didn't exist and talked myself out of doing things because I was convinced they wouldn't go well. If you're my lawyer or surgeon, I want you to think about and plan for every possibility, but otherwise, I've learned that approach is generally a massive waste of time, energy, and attention that only makes my worries stronger.

Professionally, an area where I see people talking themselves out of starting is sleep, specifically falling asleep. I've treated those as young as six and as old as eighty-six, all of whom freak themselves out over the fear that they aren't going to be able to fall asleep. Their heads are full of elaborate worry stories that all sound the same: *"What if I can't fall asleep, I'm up all night and am so exhausted tomorrow that something terrible happens?"* Or *"What if this cycle never ends and I can't fall asleep again and this exhausted feeling lasts forever?"* Then, they start googling (not the six-year-old) how much sleep one actually needs a night, the best ways to fall asleep, what to do if you can't fall asleep, signs something is wrong if you can't fall asleep, and what sleep aids help with insomnia.

At bedtime, they have their lavender oil on and their white noise purring. They've meditated and turned off all their devices. But when they haven't fallen asleep within ten minutes, they're in a near panic. They think, "HOW COME THIS ISN'T WORK-ING? WHY AREN'T I ASLEEP? I'M NEVER GOING TO FALL ASLEEP" as they stare at the clock. All their attention is on falling asleep, an outcome they cannot control, and one they are unintentionally making more difficult for themselves. They're tired the next day and then become even more worried, concerned about whether they'll be able to fall asleep the next night. That's exactly what they then worry about all day the next day.

They replay their routine from the previous night and assess what they could do differently (in other words, they google some more). All of this attention and fear around falling asleep is fuel for your insomnia. You are unintentionally sending the message to your mind with all the thinking, googling, and worrying that falling asleep is dangerous, so your brain will respond with more worry, vigilance, and adrenaline at bedtime, making it much harder to sleep. It's like you're stuck in a hole, but you just keep digging.

I don't know if you caught this, but another reason this person can't sleep is because all their attention is on the outcome: falling asleep. The more we focus on the outcome, the further we get from actually doing it.

Instead, if we can accept that our bodies know how to sleep (if we can let them be) and focus on the process— only being in bed when we are exhausted, no screens in bed, get out of bed if you can't sleep and go into another room to read—that's focusing on the process. That's focusing on doing sleep differently.

If you find yourself bleeding before you're cut, here are some tips that can be helpful:

NOTICE THAT YOU'RE FUTURE TRIPPING

It's important to remember that all that *mishegoss* (Yiddish for craziness) you're doing in your head is making the worry stronger. It's the reason you're having so many worry thoughts. Anticipatory anxiety is not a sign of anything. Your thoughts are not predictions. The way you feel doesn't "mean" anything other than you're experiencing an emotion. It's all simply part of your worry story. The more you engage with it, the more real, important, and urgent it will feel. Sometimes it will feel so real that you will confuse your imaginary story with what's actually happening and start acting to prevent something that won't actually happen (doom-buying sleep products, worrying about what you'll do if you can't sleep, or replaying the previous night).

GET YOURSELF IN THE PRESENT

What do you see, hear, smell, taste, and feel under you? Every time your brain wants to take you out of the present, it's a matter of gently bringing it back, as you would a mini-sheepadoodle that's escaped from the backyard.

PRACTICE THE ALLOW PRINCIPLE

What's more helpful is to acknowledge that right now, you're feeling worried, and it doesn't mean anything about the future. You're making an intentional decision not to engage with worry thoughts. Using the "can't sleep" example from above, you can inject back into your mind the fact that your body knows how to sleep, and you've (ultimately) fallen asleep every night of your life thus far, so the less you get involved, the better. ALLOW. Get back to work while the feeling is there. There's no need to do anything more about it.

WINS

CHAPTER 18

MISHAP #9

Heat Is On, Mind Goes Blank

H as this ever happened to you? You planned out how you wanted to approach someone about a sticky situation. You thought about what you wanted to say, maybe even wrote it out, but once you got there or they said something to you first, you got nervous and couldn't remember anything you were planning to say? It happens to me with some frequency. The soliloquy I rehearsed goes out the window, and I impulsively say something I regret. Maybe I give TMI (so awkward) or am a bitch or say something generally not helpful to the situation.

Nothing that happens in this scenario is surprising. When we get outside our window of tolerance, our brains want to escape or avoid. In plain English, when we get overwhelmed, we cannot remember shit. We go into fight or flight mode, so we can't access our problem-solving and thinking brains. I don't know about you, but I don't remember ninety-nine percent of the acronyms I read in books, which is why I hesitated to create one when I coined The ALLOW Principle. If I'm the least bit anxious, there's a zero percent chance I'm going to remember it without prompting. I know enough about the brain to know this is typical, but I hear clients interpret that experience as:

- I'm not meant to make this change.
- It's too hard or too much.
- I just "can't remember" anything.
- It's not meant to be ("it" being whatever change they're trying to make).

They then back out of doing something and reinforce the perception that there is a sensation they can't tolerate. Which is likely not true.

Here's my very basic understanding of Lisa Feldman Barrett's research on the brain and why we do what we've always done. First, who is Lisa? According to her website, she is "among the top one percent most cited scientists in the world for revolutionary research in psychology and neuroscience." Basically, she is the Beyoncé of the intersection of neuroscience and psychology. A point she reiterates in her book, *How Emotions are Made,* is that it is metabolically inefficient for the brain to learn something new, which is why it can feel exhausting when we're undertaking new activities. If left to its own devices, the brain will assume you will do what you've always done (the path of least resistance) and prepare you for that. If you want to do something different, you have to be very intentional about the change. Toward that end, here are some approaches that can help:

- Assume you'll forget and be prepared.
- Use Post-it Notes to remind yourself.
- Put reminders everywhere of the change you're trying to make.
- Slow down when you get triggered. Intentionally move more slowly so you respond to the situation and not your feelings.
- Try to be proactive about challenging situations (go on the offense).

WINS

CHAPTER 19

MISHAP #10
Using Feelings as a Fallback

This mishap occurs when we use how we feel as a reason not to do something. Most of us are familiar with having moments where we feel too stressed out or too anxious to push ourselves, but I also hear a lot of people say they don't want to do "the thing" in a given moment because they don't want to "ruin their good mood (or vibe)."

Susan was referred to me by another client. She said she needed someone who was an expert in "thought transformation." I didn't think I fit the bill but trusted the client who referred her, so I was willing to give it a go.

Susan struggled with unpleasant intrusive thoughts about hurting someone, which terrified her.

Because they scared her, she would do anything to get rid of them and avoid having them happen to begin with, which, for her, meant trying to keep her mind busy all the time. Not knowing these thoughts were normal *or* how to respond to them, she also tried lots of unhelpful interventions like thought replacement ("No, I'd never do that!") and thought suppression ("Stop thinking that!"). Not surprisingly nothing was working, and she felt like she was on a hamster wheel, trying to get rid of the thoughts but then having them continue to pop up.

Because several influencers she followed hyped up their programs' ability to combat this sort of thinking, she had spent tens of thousands of dollars (and she was not a wealthy woman) on life coaching, masterminds, and workshops promising to help her "step into her power," get out of her way, and choose what thoughts she wanted instead of the thoughts that kept popping up. Because she was taught that she could "manifest abundance" through her thinking, when her thoughts were unpleasant, she was terrified.

Because she was scared of these thoughts, she didn't want to do anything that could trigger her to have them. That meant that being in the right vibe at all times was really important. She would do a "vibe check" (her words) of her environment, the people she was with, and her internal state. If she felt even the slightest sensations when she first started, she would cancel plans, "just in case."

If she didn't like the "energy" in a place, she would leave (even if that meant leaving a medical office minutes prior to an appointment). If she didn't get a good feeling about a medical provider, she immediately switched. She even wanted to control the vibe of therapy by finding a therapist who could "just keep it positive."

I was very direct that what she saw as her solution—avoiding feeling any distress or discomfort—had clearly become her problem. She agreed, yet she still wanted the kind of therapy she wanted, so it wasn't a good fit for us to work together.

Fast forward a year (and $10,000 more spent/wasted on interventions that didn't work). She had run out of options and was *still* having intrusive thoughts. It's a common story. She reached back out, more willing to give my approach a try than she was the year prior.

When we started treatment, things initially went okay. The between-session work didn't trigger her distress or discomfort. Once it started to get harder, however, that changed. She began agreeing to engage in situations/experiences that could, and likely would, impact her mood. Initially, her reason for bailing (her excuse) was that she was feeling "too good" to do it; "What kind of therapy would intentionally want someone's mood to get worse?" Then, her rationale became that she was "too stressed" or "too anxious" to do the work. The story she told herself was that doing the exposure homework would make her so uncomfortable that the entire day (or perhaps, days, if not weeks) might be ruined. She didn't think she could handle that, so she avoided it.

As often happens, she started having unwanted thoughts when she was feeling good, so her mood was getting ruined either way. That gave me the foothold I needed to have her reconsider doing her exposure homework. At least if we did it this way, she would be "on the offense" and intentionally going after the distress instead of being in a defensive position, as she had been. Once she started, she saw more clearly that the story she'd created in her head about how something would go was way worse than what actually happened. Yes, facing her uncomfortable thoughts of wanting to harm someone head-on was scary, but she learned that her worst fears never came true, and the intensity of her feelings didn't overwhelm her. She learned that she would be anxious and uncomfortable for a period of time, and then it would pass. Life did not have to stop. In fact, it passed faster when she continued living and acting *with* all her feelings.

Susan emailed me about a year after she finished treatment to tell me it had been a year since she unfollowed all the "influencers," and she'd never felt better. She finally felt like she was living a full life, and when unpleasant thoughts popped up, she'd learned to treat them like junk mail and move on. Her mood was no longer the sole determinant of the actions she took. And, my personal favorite outcome, she got rid of the "Good vibes Only" word art in her house.

So what brilliant words did I use to turn things around for Susan? There likely were none. Ultimately, it was a leap of faith on *her* part to see what would actually happen if she allowed her thoughts—even when she was feeling good. In this work, we intentionally go after whatever we've been avoiding. In this case, it was Susan's thoughts of harming someone. She absolutely had no intention of doing so; these were unwanted, intrusive thoughts that she was trying to suppress and avoid. Her homework, therefore, was to intentionally (and often) think these thoughts in order to practice responding differently to the feelings. It's critical to do the homework regardless of how you're feeling that day, and she struggled with this at first because she didn't want to do the homework when she felt good. She worried it might ruin her day.

But when she actually did it, she saw that the process wasn't nearly as bad as her worry had her believing it would be, and that gave her the willingness to keep trying, which built momentum and confidence. Through action, she was able to rewrite her story.

If you find yourself falling into the "But I'm too anxious/happy/stressed/scared/frustrated/overwhelmed" trap, remember:

Behavior changes perception much faster than

the other way around.

Ask yourself:

- What is the smallest step I can take toward my goal?
- How long can I commit to doing it?

Once you determine the answers, take that next step. Hesitation breeds anxiety, so commit and execute. It's easier to build momentum after you've gotten started, and visualizing how you'll feel when you're finished is often an incredible motivator.

As I advise of my clients all the time: Try not to measure progress by how you feel or what thoughts are in your head. Measure progress by how you *respond* to those things.

You never want to base progress on something you cannot control (e.g., how you feel and what thoughts pop up). This is especially true when you're first starting out and may feel worse before you feel better. You want to measure progress based on something over which you have agency—your behaviors (e.g., your response to your thoughts and feelings).

WINS

CHAPTER 20

The Doing
(AND THE INCREDIBLE PAYOFF)

I hope that, because you've made it this far, you have a better understanding of what's been holding you back and how you can apply some new tools (including self-compassion) to move forward in a more effective way.

And now the real work starts: the doing.

The irony is not lost on me that the title of this book is *Just Do Nothing*, and I'm now recommending that you go *do* the things you want (or need) to do regardless of how you feel (obviously assuming you're safe in the process). The entire point of Just Do Nothing is that, for so many people, it's time to *do* differently. It's time to do less in order to gain more.

I've given you a series of principles to follow as well as several proven strategies for getting out of your head so you can get out of your way. I've also provided, perhaps to your chagrin, as many analogies and examples as I can.

By this point, it's a good sign if you:

- Have a basic understanding of why, when it comes to distress and discomfort, we want to do what's counterintuitive.
- Have some practice tolerating distress and understanding why this is important.
- Are practicing the mental fitness skills regularly.
- Are practicing mental fitness outside of planned times (in clinical terms, this is "generalizing the process").
- Have done your readiness exercise and made an honest assessment.
- Have created your Sliding Scale of Distress for a specific change you desire to make.
- Practiced The ALLOW Principle with a low-distress experience/situation.

If you've done all of that, I'm *so* impressed. If you haven't, I suggest completing the above before moving on. Once you feel you understand what it means to relax into distress or discomfort as you do a specific behavior, I encourage you to take the next step on your scale. Work on that step *daily*, multiple times a day if you can, until it gets easier. Once your confidence with that situation/experience increases, move on to the next one. Generally, I give my clients a week to practice each step on the scale. The more often they engage with the particular step they're on, the better. With every repetition, you are strengthening that pathway. It's the best way to create new learning and start building momentum in a more positive direction.

It may be hard to fathom all that awaits you when you learn to do distress and discomfort differently. Most of my clients come to see me for one perceived challenge and leave with a life that has opened up in many ways, to many opportunities.

Larry is a typical example. He left me a reluctant voicemail in the fall of 2020. He was calling at the strong urging of his wife, because he was, apparently, driving everyone crazy with his Covid worries. He wanted to make it clear that he wasn't convinced he had a problem, but to placate his wife, he agreed to call.

When I asked if he could *briefly* give me an example of what might be bugging his wife, he told me how he wanted everyone in the family to strip down in the garage and shower every time he, his wife, or any of their three kids entered the house. He had even converted part of the garage to a "bathroom" for their decontamination. **Let me be clear: Larry and his family were not in a high-risk group, nor did they have contact with anyone in a high-risk group, and these were not the CDC recommendations at the time.** Engaging in these precautions (and there were *many* more) simply made him *feel* safer.

I wasn't convinced I was the right fit or that he was on board and didn't need more help than I could offer. Nevertheless, we were both willing to give it a try. We spent many sessions working on reasons for him to change and reasons for him not to. It wasn't until his seven-year-old daughter started washing her hands until they bled that he began to question things. All of his excuses about the kids being "too young to notice my quirks," declarations that "they're not picking up on anything," and reminders that "handwashing is recommended in a pandemic" stopped working. Eventually, he came around to working on his excessive fears around Covid exposure and transmission. He learned that the more out of control he felt on the inside, the more he tried to control the outside. All the washing of the clothes, bodies, hands, mouths, mail, packages, and groceries was an effort to get rid of all the distress and discomfort he felt about what was happening around him.

Over the course of the next six months, he gradually cut out all of the behaviors that were over and above the CDC recommendations and allowed whatever thoughts, feelings, and sensations that came up to come and go. It was hard work. He had to remind himself that he could be scared but not be in danger. And when the family got Covid, which was his biggest fear, he learned that he coped better than he would have predicted. It required a lot of courage, patience, and faith in the process, and he certainly commented more than once that it was mentally exhausting but ultimately well worth it.

For me, one of the coolest parts was when he would notice other areas where he was avoiding feeling something. He would start saying things in session like, "I noticed that I immediately grabbed my phone because I was embarrassed" or "I know I gave in right away because I didn't want her to be upset with me" or "I think my wife avoids her own discomfort by over-scheduling herself." The more confident he became in trying things, regardless of how he might feel, the more inclined he was to change his behavior in other areas. Now he was willing to work on setting appropriate limits with his kids and have them stick to a consistent bedtime routine. At work, he was more open to having difficult conversations with his colleagues. With his wife, he wasn't asking for reassurance about what he should do and constantly asking if she was okay. He practiced being "sure enough" and believing she would speak up if she needed to.

An unexpected bonus was that he lost weight when he stopped "stress snacking." Once we terminated our work together after a year, he had worked through Covid fears, parenting issues, *and* ineffective communication patterns. Larry learned a process for responding to the stuff in his head so he could focus on what mattered. In reflection, he said it was the hardest thing he'd ever done, and this is from someone who completed graduate school, runs businesses, has three kids, and runs marathons.

Seeing someone's world open up like this is,

undoubtedly, the best part of my job. It sounds cheesy, I know, but it's true. Obviously, I cannot predict what's on the other side for you once you learn how to approach discomfort and distress differently, but here are the common things I hear and see people becoming capable of:

- Being more flexible
- Being more resilient
- Being able to do things spontaneously
- Being able to do things because they want to, not because they feel like they have to
- Not micromanaging their thoughts all day
- Not trying to control how they feel
- Not trying to control how other people feel
- Having more time to do things
- Being able to trust themselves again
- Making decisions faster
- Having more money
- Having more fun
- Being more present
- Having better relationships
- Having days that aren't planned based on how they feel or fear they'll feel
- Not feeling controlled by how they feel
- Not being scared of their feelings
- Their mood isn't dependent on how other people feel or their moods
- Their life begins to open up again

I could go on and on with client stories, but now I want you to go out and make your own. And when you do, let me know how it goes.

I believe in you, and I'm rooting for you.

ACKNOWLEDGEMENTS

This book would have stayed an idea in my head had it not been for the unwavering support of Jenn Prochaska, who has helped me grow my business and find my voice. With thanks...

To my book coach, editor, and publisher, Elizabeth Lyons, who made this process as transparent and fun as it could possibly be.

To Drew Linsalata, who introduced me to Elizabeth, and has been on the distress tolerance bandwagon with me since my interest was piqued.

To Georgie Gray, who workshopped titles with me over brunches and discussions of Jewish Matchmaking. She also introduced me to my amazing publicist, Sarah Wilson.

To my eldest daughter, Izzy, who copy edited, was on the title committee, and let me bounce ideas off her as she finished her senior year of college.

To my friends who have been there through thick and thin.

To my kids, I cannot find words to describe how much I love you and how you brighten even the darkest of days.

To my amazing parents whose unwavering support has been the through-line of my life, thank you.

ABOUT THE AUTHOR

Joanna Hardis, LISW-S, is a cognitive behavioral therapist based in Cleveland, Ohio. Committed to using evidence-based treatments, Joanna helps people get "unstuck." Through her private practice as well as virtual workshops on distress tolerance, Joanna shows people how to respond to being uncomfortable by giving them the knowledge and tools they need to move forward. She may drop a favorite Yiddish word (or two) during a session, and her goal is always for her clients not to need her anymore.

She has been quoted in *The Today Show, Self,* and *Well and Good* magazines.

She received her B.S. at Cornell University and her M.S.S.A. at Case Western Reserve University. She earned her certification from the Cleveland Center for Cognitive Therapy in 2000, SPACE (Supportive Counseling for Anxious Childhood Emotions) Certification in 2016, and she's one of a handful of clinicians with the highest training in Exposure and Response Prevention for OCD in Northeast Ohio.

In her spare time, Joanna enjoys powerlifting, doing anything with her three kids, traveling, and getting sucked into bad reality TV.

www.JoannaHardis.com

Made in the USA
Columbia, SC
03 September 2024

41575156R00140